digital diagrams

D1277785

HUMBER COLLEGE L.R.C. (LAKESHORE)

digital diagrams

TREVOR BOUNFORD

SERIES CONSULTANT
ALASTAIR CAMPBELL

HUMBER COLLEGE
LAKESHORE CAMPUS
LEARNING RESOURCE CENTRE
3199 LAKESHORE BLVD WEST
TORONTO, ONTARIO M8V 1K8

**WATSON-GUPTILL
PUBLICATIONS**
New York

To Sheila, Eleanor, Hannah, and Felix

First published in the United States in 2000 by Watson-Guptill Publications, a division of BPI Communications, Inc., 770 Broadway, New York, NY 10003

Copyright © 2000 The Ivy Press Limited and Alastair Campbell

All rights reserved. No part of this book may be reproduced or used in any form or by any means—graphic, electronic, or mechanical, including photocopying, recording, taping, or information storage and retrieval systems—without written permission of the publisher.

Trademarks and trademark names are used throughout this book to describe and inform you about various proprietary products. Such mention is intended to benefit the owner of the trademark and is not intended to infringe copyright nor to imply any claim to the mark other than that made by its owner.

The information contained in this book is given without warranty and, while every precaution has been taken in compiling the book, neither the author nor publisher assume any responsibility or liability whatsoever to any person or entity with respect to any errors which may exist in the book, nor for any loss of data which may occur as the result of such errors, or for the efficacy or performance of any product or process described in the book.

Library of Congress Catalog Card Number: 00-105597

ISBN 0-8230-1572-6

This book was conceived, designed, and produced by Alastair Campbell and The Ivy Press Limited
The Old Candlemakers
West Street, Lewes
East Sussex BN7 2NZ

Editorial Director:
Sophie Collins
Art Director:
Peter Bridgewater
Editor:
Peter Leek
Designers:
Trevor Bounford and Alastair Campbell
Illustrations:
Denise Goodey, Nicholas Rowland, Helen Humphries and the late Bob Chapman. Particular thanks to Denise Goodey for frequent heroic efforts and to Bruce Robertson for his brutal encouragement. Thanks also to Sarah Lubikowski and Stephen Coulson for help in the early stages.

Originated and printed by Hong Kong Graphic, Hong Kong

INTRODUCTION

We seem to live in an information-driven world. No political statement, company policy, or marketing strategy is considered valid without a suitably bulging packet of statistical analysis to support it. Indeed, society seems to have an insatiable appetite for information. However, information in its raw form is largely indigestible for anyone but the specialist. According to Seurat, "nature needs a little cooking"; and so it is with data. The same digital technology that has enabled the glut of data can also be harnessed to distribute it in an appetizing and (informatively) nutritious way. However, although any number of software packages now seem capable of producing data in some graphic format, the expertise that is needed to turn a stew of facts into an appealing display of digestible information is not so readily available. Over the years there have been master chefs in the art of information design. William Playfair and Willard Brinton were great innovators in their time. More recently we have Otto Neurath's Isotype Institute and Bruce Robertson's Diagram Group.

This book is aimed at the nonspecialist, the general cook who needs to prepare some specialist dishes. It is, in a way, a recipe book, a book of practical menus. It is a guidebook, a reference book for practical use aimed at pragmatic users. It is not an academic analysis of the subject, nor is it a step-by-step manual for the novice. Apart from the historical examples in Section 1 and one or two items in the illustrative diagrams section, all the images have been created digitally. I have assumed that readers will have a reasonable level of competence in computer usage. The book is crammed with as much guidance, as many words and visual examples, as is sensible in a book of this size and I believe that it will serve to inform and inspire most users. *Bon appetit!*

Trevor Bounford
Cambridge

WHAT IS A DIAGRAM?

Deciding what is and what is not a diagram may seem an easy, and perhaps pointless, exercise. However, in order to compile a book about information design, it is important to determine where the vague, and subjective, border might lie. Bar and pie charts, line graphs, and other statistical charts are obviously included, as are organizational charts. I also count symbols and icons as valid candidates; there is similarly no problem with timelines; and tables qualify, despite often being largely typographic designs. Most of the borderline cases are, in fact, relational and illustrative diagrams.

When they are cross-sections, exploded or ghosted drawings, or labeled illustrations, illustration-based diagrams are clearly identifiable as diagrams. But what of pure illustration—unlabeled, representational art? If the art is designed in such a way that it, literally, illustrates one or more points of information, or if it is part of a sequence that sets out to do that, I count it as an illustrative diagram. If it merely records a scene, then for the purposes of this book it is an illustration.

For present purposes, I also have a cut-off point for relational diagrams. I've excluded cartography in its conventional form, as found in general atlases, road maps, maritime charts, star charts, and so on. But I do include maps, plans, and charts that are designed to address specific information-dissemination tasks. Also, if a map or chart has unique design qualities, I count it as information design, distinguishing it from the kind of standard cartography that is merely the application of an established language. However, I have tried to indicate the importance of the standard cartographic conventions.

In this book, diagrams have been grouped under five headings—illustrative diagrams, statistical diagrams, relational diagrams, organizational diagrams, and time charts. But these categories overlap, and they are often combined in individual charts.

GEBURTEN UND STERBEFÄLLE IN WIEN

1912-15

1916-19

1920-23

1924-27

Jedes Kind = 20.000 Lebendgeburten   Jeder Sarg = 20.000 Sterbefälle

Above A bar chart composed of icons. Designed in the late 1920s by the Isotype Institute. Although composed of illustrative items, this is clearly a statistical diagram.

MOVING ABOUT THE LINE

Do not walk on the line unless you must. Where there is an authorised route – use it. If you have to walk on the line, keep clear of the tracks whenever possible, and face the direction from which trains approach. Give careful thought to this and make sure that you consider the various possibilities.

WRONG *Walking in the direction of traffic*

RIGHT *In the cess and well clear*

3

RIGHT *Standing clear*

Wherever you are on the track, it will always pay you to look around and to weigh up your position. Remember that diesel and electric trains and locomotives differ from steam locomotives in several important ways –

> they approach quietly at all speeds
> there is no smoke or steam
> there is little vibration of the rails
> they accelerate quickly

Stand well away from any passing train – otherwise you may be hurt by a loose sheet end, or by a sheet-tie, or by a piece of coal or some other object falling from the train.

Keep well clear of trains passing over detonators, or you might be hit by flying pieces of metal.

When on the line, don't get so absorbed in talking with your mates that you neglect your safety – and theirs.

WRONG   *The conversation may be necessary but it is not in the right place*

5

Left Pages from a safety training manual. More than mere pictures. The color highlighting makes the point in these illustrative diagrams.

ILLUSTRATIVE DIAGRAMS

The term illustrative diagram encompasses a broad spectrum—from simple symbolic icons through to complex cross-sections. Some categories of illustrative diagram (architectural, anatomical, scientific, engineering drawing, and so on) are too specialized to be covered in a book like this. The varieties included here are of the type the information designer is likely to encounter most frequently. Even so, many of them will call for the special skills of a trained illustrator, or need access to a comprehensive source of professionally produced clip art that can be digitally manipulated to suit the designer's requirements. Although other types of chart (statistical and organizational diagrams, for example) often include pictorial elements, illustrative diagrams make use of the image itself to describe the situation or events shown. They are generally used to portray physical rather than abstract concepts, and they almost invariably deal with a localized context.

10

Fig. 249.—WITH SIX BEARERS.

Figs. 247–249.—Lift.

(The patient on the knees of Nos. 1, 2, and 3 bearers, the bearers on the right disengaged and standing up [having stepped back one pace] and the bearer nearest the patient supplying the stretcher).

Above Illustration from the eighth edition of *First Aid to the Sick and Injured*, published in 1913. A highly detailed figure drawing with arrows and labels conveys the instruction.

11

Above Diagrams from a book on italic lettering by Gerard Mercator, published in 1540. The drawings show the right and wrong way to hold the quill for lettering on maps.

TABLES AND GRAPHS

Statistical diagrams are used to enable comparisons of data to be made. In this book, statistical diagrams have been subdivided into the categories of tables, line and scatter graphs, and bar, area, and volume charts.

In basic tables the data is set out on a matrix or grid, so that numerical values can be read against category headings. In effect, the table is a set of lists that can be read horizontally or vertically, the user being required to assimilate and assess the values. For convenience, the table section of this book includes nondata tables. These function in much the same way—the difference being that, instead of numerical values, some or all of the table entries are verbal statements or else visual symbols that represent words.

Line graphs make use of a different grid matrix. Each string or list of data is plotted against two intersecting axes. Commonly the horizontal (x) axis represents even divisions of time, and the vertical (y) axis shows values.

12

TABLE I—REACH

Case	DESCRIPTION	Distance Moved Inches	LEVELED TIME T. M. U.					
			A Std.	A Hand In Motion	A with C D or B	B Hand In Motion	C or D	E
A	Reach to object in fixed location, or to object in other hand or on which other hand rests.	1	1.8	1.3	2.1	1.5	3.6	1.7
		2	3.7	2.8	4.3	2.7	5.9	3.8
		3	5.0	3.8	5.9	3.6	7.3	5.3
		4	6.1	4.9	7.1	4.3	8.4	6.8
B	Reach to single object in location which may vary slightly from cycle to cycle.	5	6.5	5.3	7.8	5.0	9.4	7.4
		6	7.0	5.7	8.6	5.7	10.1	8.0
		7	7.4	6.1	9.3	6.5	10.8	8.7
		8	7.9	6.5	10.1	7.2	11.5	9.3
C	Reach to object in group.	9	8.3	6.9	10.8	7.9	12.2	9.9
		10	8.7	7.3	11.5	8.6	12.9	10.5
		12	9.6	8.1	12.9	10.1	14.2	11.8
		14	10.5	8.9	14.4	11.5	15.6	13.0
D	Reach to very small object or where accurate grasp is required.	16	11.4	9.7	15.8	12.9	17.0	14.2
		18	12.3	10.5	17.2	14.4	18.4	15.5
		20	13.1	11.3	18.6	15.8	19.8	16.7
E	Reach to indefinite location to get hand in position for body balance or next motion or out of way.	22	14.0	12.1	20.1	17.3	21.2	18.0
		24	14.9	12.9	21.5	18.8	22.5	19.2
		26	15.8	13.7	22.9	20.2	23.9	20.4
		28	16.7	14.5	24.4	21.7	25.3	21.7
		30	17.5	15.3	25.8	23.2	26.7	22.9

Left Table from a methods/time measurement system developed in the 1940s. Well-ordered type sets out technical detail so that it may be easily assimilated.

A line connects each of the data points on the graph, and the angle of each line segment indicates the degree of change between the values.

Each line of a line graph must represent variations of the value of an item or a collective group of items. It would be misleading, even nonsensical, to construct a line graph with each data point representing a different category. The data points must be a linear string, so that neighboring points have a valid proximity.

Scatter graphs (*see page 52*) are also based on two axes—but instead of a linear string, the values are for individual items and the points are not connected by lines. It is the interrelationship of the various points that is significant, rather than the progressive comparison of the line graph.

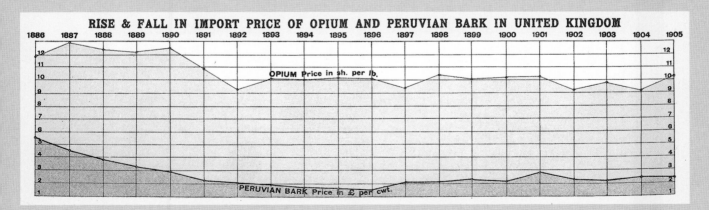

Above Line graph from *Atlas of the World's Commerce*, published in 1907. A straightforward line graph which is more interesting for its content than for its treatment.

BAR, AREA, AND VOLUME CHARTS

The three other varieties of statistical diagrams found in this book are the bar chart, the area chart, and the volume chart. These portray the values of items as length (in bar charts), area, or volume. In effect, they display values in one, two, or three dimensions. Whereas bar charts and area charts are shown in their entirety in a two-dimensional drawing (either in print or on screen), volume charts have to convey the concept of the third dimension within the constraints of two dimensions.

Unlike the line graph, which presents a sequential review of the value of a single item or category, the bar chart has the flexibility to represent a series of different (but comparable) items. For example, a bar chart could show the price of a commodity at defined points over a given period of time. Or it could show the price of the same commodity over the same period but in different locations. Or it could show the prices of a range of commodities in a given place or over a given period,

14

ACTUAL HEIGHTS
(in America, Australia, etc.)

	Feet
Aconcagua (Argentina)	23,081
Sorata (Bolivia)	21,700
Chimborazo (Ecuador)	20,810
Mt. McKinley (Alaska)	20,300
Orizaba (Mexico)	18,200
Mt. St. Elias (Canada)	18,024
Sa. de Santa Marta (Colombia)	16,700
Sierra Merida (Venezuela)	15,400
Mt. Whitney (California)	14,500
Mt. Rainier (Washington)	14,363
Long's Peak (Colorado)	14,270
Vol. Fuego (Guatemala)	13,980
Mt. Waddington (Brit. Columbia)	13,260
Mt. Cook (New Zealand)	12,349
Ruapehu (New Zealand)	9,175
Roraima (Venezuela)	8,530
Sa. Maestra (Cuba)	8,400
Koskiusko (N.S.W.)	7,328
Allegheny Mt.s (United States)	6,711
White Mts. (United States)	6,286

ACTUAL HEIGHTS
(in Europe, Asia and Africa)

	Feet
Everest (Nepal)	29,002
Godwin Austen (Kashmir)	28,250
Pamir (Central Asia)	25,760
Hindu Kush (Afghanistan)	25,400
Tien Shan (Central Asia)	22,802
Kwen Lun (Tibet)	22,370
Kilimanjaro (Tanganyika)	19,324
Elburz (Persia)	18,600
Elbruz (Russia)	18,530
Ruwenzori (Uganda)	16,794
Mont Blanc (France)	15,780
Atlas (Morocco)	15,420
Owen Stanley Ra. (New Guinea)	13,200
Drakensberg (South Africa)	12,000
Pyrenees (Spain)	11,170
Mt. Etna (Sicily)	10,870
Carpathians (Central Europe)	8,740
Mt. Doré (France)	6,190
Ural Mts. (Russia)	5,430
Ben Nevis (Scotland)	4,406

and so on. It is this flexibility that makes it particularly useful as an information-design tool.

Area charts and volume charts share this flexibility. Their particular advantage is that they can accommodate a greater range of values. A linear value of 100 units is only 10 times the length of a linear value of 10—but an area of 100 units is the equivalent of 10 units across by 10 high, and a volume measuring 10 across by 10 high by 10 deep represents a value of 1000.

The most common form of area chart is the pie chart, which, in its most basic form, is just a radially divided circle. Volume charts are used much less frequently than area charts, even though modern digital technology facilitates accurate three-dimensional plotting.

15

Left Elaborate bar chart from the 1934 *Daily Mail* edition of *Philip's Universal Atlas*. Produced for a popular, and probably relatively young, readership, this diagram is designed to stimulate interest.

AIR FLEETS OF THE WORLD *

United States 1,752

France 1,687

Russia 1,500

Japan 1,384

Great Britain 838

Yugoslavia 627

Rumania 599

Czechoslovakia 546

Spain 462

Canada 355

✱ "First Line" Military Aeroplanes

Left Area chart, also from the 1934 *Daily Mail* edition of *Philip's Universal Atlas*. Here again, a diagram with a strong visual impact draws the reader's attention.

RELATIONAL DIAGRAMS

There are two kinds of diagrams that illustrate the relationship of non-quantitative items. Relational diagrams show the relative positions of things that are either at fixed locations in the physical world or are planned to be at fixed locations (whereas organizational diagrams illustrate the conceptual interrelationship of physical or non-physical entities regardless of their geographical location).

Signs, plans, maps, and charts all provide a graphic indication or representation of location. They enable a user to relate to places, and to relate those places to each other. In one form or another, maps have existed for thousands of years. Made from bark, hide, bamboo, papyrus, or other durable materials, they have enabled humans to travel great distances. Early maps of the world may lack precision in measurement, but in concept they are remarkably accurate. Even the stars have been mapped from early times, as an aid to navigation.

Signs along routes—originally temporary mounds of pebbles, but later permanent objects, painted or carved with names and distances—are relational implements. The modern equivalent, the highway indicator with a variable digital display, is the current version of a prehistoric visual tool.

Digital technology allows more sophisticated and more accurate representation, yet by their very nature relational diagrams are inevitably a compromise. They are a reduction of the physical world to a manageable but recognizable visual form. For the sake of clarity and functional efficiency, not all detail can be included. The reality has to be edited, and it is the information designer's function to make editorial decisions that will result in a plan, map, or chart that fulfills its function by aiding, and not hindering, the user.

Right and above
Sections of maps from *Grosser Weltatlas der Büchergilde*, published in 1963. A wide variety of highly stylized treatments intended to maintain interest throughout a large volume of diagrams and maps.

Right Map of the heavens in August, September, and October, from Milner's *Gallery of Nature*, published in 1855. An immensely detailed hand-engraving.

ORGANIZATIONAL DIAGRAMS

We live in a world of complex social structures—local, national, and international governments and institutions, multinational commercial enterprises, non-governmental organizations, and so on. Organizational diagrams are needed to explain the complex and often convoluted links within and between these structures.

There are numerous applications for organizational charts. The family tree is a commonly used and relatively simple form. It sets out the lines of descent through two or (usually) more generations. Complex versions may weave together lines from several families. Charts of the same type are frequently used to plot the corporate interminglings of commercial enterprises resulting from mergers and takeovers.

Organizational charts are also used to explain or summarize cyclical flow and interaction—for example, to describe the natural water cycle, a continuous process with no beginning and (hopefully) no end.

Unlike relational diagrams, which deal only with physical items, organizational diagrams can be used to show the relationship of activities, concepts, or abstract items. They can also, in the form of flow charts, be used to describe stages in a process.

Diagnostic charts (a type of organizational chart able to encompass abstract processes—such as thoughts and feelings) plot a course of considerations or alternative "routes," determined by answers to questions embedded within the chart.

The Tree of Life

Left The Tree of Life, from *The Wonderful Story of the Human Body*, by "A Well Known Physician." A simple organization chart reducing a complex structure to a simple visual analogy.

Right Organizational diagram designed by the Isotype Institute in 1947 for *How Do You Do Tovarish?*, published by Adprint Ltd/George Harrap and Co. Ltd. The Isotype Institute set out to convey information with the minimum amount of "written" language.

Opportunity in the Soviet Union

TIME CHARTS

Time may be portrayed visually in a number of ways. Generally we perceive time as a linear progression. Indeed, the term "timeline," denoting a linear visual record of events, derives from this perception. But time can also be cyclical, with recurring events following a circular pattern. We also use the table matrix to visualize time in diaries, calendars, and timetables.

All of these visualizations are valid, and each has its own uses and context. It is informative to plot the course of historical events along a linear path, particularly when making comparisons over a period of time—the changing fortunes of different civilizations, for example, or phases of development or cultural activity within a single civilization. Timetables list a series of comparative options, with the time progression shown along both the horizontal and vertical axes. Cyclical events can be shown on a circular grid (seasonal activity following a natural cycle particularly lends itself to this).

20

Soviet Working Week

Each red unit represents 1 hour of work
blue: Sundays   green: free days

Right Time chart designed by the Isotype Institute, from *How Do You Do Tovarish?*, published in 1947 by Adprint Ltd/ George Harrap and Co. Ltd. Information is simplified to a visual pattern that can be readily assimilated.

Right Time chart from *Graphic Methods for Presenting Facts* by Willard C. Brinton, published in 1914 by McGraw-Hill. Again, data is reduced to a visual pattern allowing the user to read detail and obtain a clear impression of the implications.

	1860	1870	1880	1890	1900	Rank
New York..	1	1	1	1	1	1 New York
Penn......	2	2	2	2	2	2 Penn.
Ohio......	3	3	3	4	4	3 Illinois
Illinois....	4	4	4	3	3	4 Ohio
Virginia....	5	8	8	8	8	5 Missouri
Indiana....	6	6	6	7	23	6 Texas
Mass......	7	7	7	23	7	7 Mass.
Missouri...	8	9	9	6	6	8 Indiana
Kentucky..	9	10	16	16	16	9 Michigan
Tennessee..	10	5	20	20	20	10 Iowa
Georgia....	11	20	23	9	11	11 Georgia
N. Carolina.	12	11	10	11	9	12 Kentucky
Alabama...	13	16	11	10	15	13 Wisconsin
Mississippi.	14	12	5	15	10	14 Tennessee
Wisconsin..	15	15	12	5	12	15 N. Carolina
Michigan...	16	13	15	12	21	16 New Jersey
Louisiana ..	17	21	13	13	5	17 Virginia
S. Carolina.	18	14	14	21	13	18 Alabama
Maryland ..	19	23	21	33	30	19 Minnesota
Iowa......	20	19	33	30	14	20 Mississippi
New Jersey.	21	17	18	14	26	21 California
Maine.....	22	18	17	26	33	22 Kansas
Texas......	23	22	19	18	17	23 Louisiana
Connecticut	24	26	26	25	25	24 S. Carolina
Arkansas...	25	24	25	17	25	25 Arkansas
California..	26	25	30	38	19	26 Maryland
N.Hampsh'e	27	41	22	19	38	27 Nebraska
Vermont...	28	30	24	41	41	28 W. Virginia
Rhode Isl'nd	29	33	41	24	24	29 Connecticut
Minnesota..	30	28	38	22	22	30 Maine
Florida	31	27	27	42	42	31 Colorado
Delaware...	32	29	28	31	31	32 Florida
Kansas	33	31	29	27	39	33 Washington
New Mexico	34	35	31	39	29	34 Rhode Isl'nd
Dist. of C..	35	32	42	29	36	35 Oregon
Oregon.....	36	38	35	28	27	36 N.Hampsh'e
Utah......	37	34	36	49	49	37 S. Dakota
Nebraska...	38	36	32	36	51	38 Oklahoma
Washington.	39	37	37	35	52	39 Indian Ter.
Nevada....	40	40	45	37	28	40 Vermont
Colorado.....		42	34	50	50	41 N. Dakota
		39	39	32	35	42 Dist. of C.
Montana.........		43	40	34	37	43 Utah
Idaho		44	46	43	43	44 Montana
Dakota...........		45	43	44	34	45 N. Mexico
Arizona...........		46	48	51	32	46 Delaware
Wyoming		47	44	47	44	47 Idaho
			46		53	48 Hawaii
				40	46	49 Arizona
				48	47	50 Wyoming
					48	51 Alaska
					40	52 Nevada

Adapted from the United States Statistical Atlas

ILLUSTRATIVE DIAGRAMS / SYMBOLS 1

Symbols, icons, graphic devices—call them what you will—these elements are a vital tool for the information designer. They can be primitive geometric shapes, refined pictograms, or anything in between. They are used to create a visual language, substituting effectively for words, and through their nonverbal form transcend normal language barriers. Sensible color application gives them even greater scope.

As with all information design, consistency of style is vital if symbols are to function effectively, particularly when several are used together. Clarity of design is also essential—ambiguity or fuzziness of thought in the design process is communicated just as easily as precision. Use the same angles, line weights, and color groups to coordinate the design style for groups of symbols, but be sure that each symbol has a clear identity and is not easily confused with any other.

24

Right Plain geometric shapes serve well as basic symbols. They will reproduce well in print at small sizes. Balance dimensions—don't necessarily make them exact. Many shapes are available to the digital designer as dingbats or typographer's sorts.

Right Combining geometric shapes is the key to simple but effective symbol design. Use the shapes as building blocks to maintain consistent treatment, but don't be too rigid. A little subtlety can add a great deal of visual sophistication. Constraining angles within a group of symbols, as well as maintaining a balance in weight, holds the group together. Remember that positive and negative also work together—space is as vital in devising symbols as it is in designing type.

Symbols have long been widely used as a substitute for written language, particularly when communication is international. Consequently, many symbols have specific accepted meanings, and should be used only in that way.

Right Road signs are a good example of geometrically based shapes with precise internationally accepted meanings. Although this limits the broader use of the shapes, it does mean that the icons are known and so need no explanation.

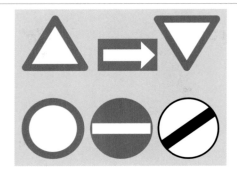

Right Some well-known symbols are subject to copyright law and may be used only with permission. These include the Olympic circles and trademarks such as the Yellow Pages fingers and the London Underground roundel.

Right Many symbols, such as these, have well-established meanings. Although these icons can be modified to suit a graphic style, the general shape must be accepted as a recognized form.

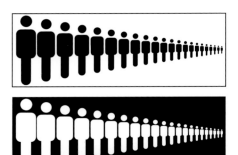

Right Flags are another obvious form of internationally recognized icon. Note that some have complex designs, and flags vary in shape. There are several collections of clip art flags, and at least one source available free on the Web.

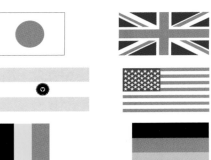

Right and below A functional symbol design must be both legible and unambiguous. Test your design at various sizes, particularly if it is for screen display—remember that users may not have a high-resolution monitor. Also, test color symbols on different backgrounds.

Right Anti-aliasing will help the visibility of small symbols. In these examples the same symbol is shown at a range of sizes with and without anti-aliasing. The enlarged samples show how the process effectively "blurs" the pixel edges.

ILLUSTRATIVE DIAGRAMS / SYMBOLS 2

Right The examples of symbol design shown here offer a range of stylization of the human form, from simple geometric shape through to near-illustrative treatment. Notice how successfully each reproduces at various sizes.

Right Here you can see a range of finishes for a symbol design. Digital reproduction and creation methods enable sophisticated use of color and line, even at small sizes.

Right The basic human-form symbols shown above can be adapted to represent variations of age and gender. Obviously, the treatments need to be consistent in style in order to create a cohesive group.

Right Accessories added to the human form create symbols representing specific activities. Keep the additions simple and in style with the general treatment—a well-placed basic shape will be more effective than a fiddly, complex rendering.

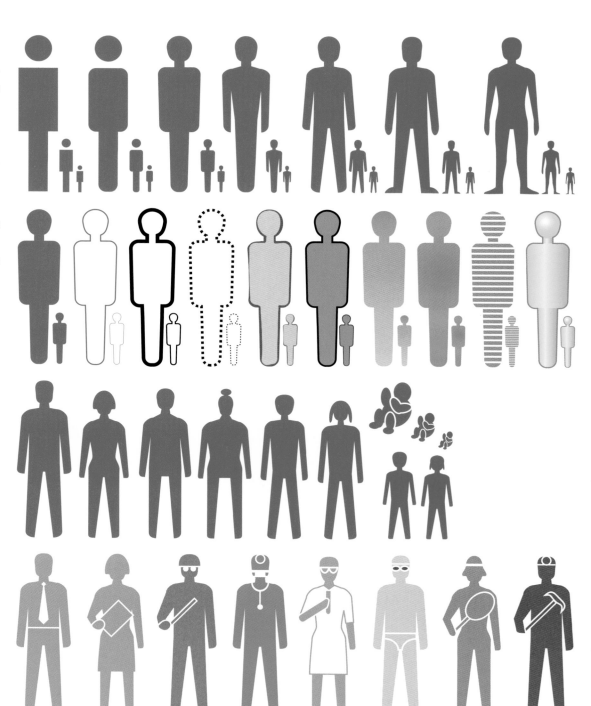

Right Use angles to suggest dynamic movement, as in these sports symbols. Once again, a few simple shapes easily suggest the appropriate accessories, which help identify the activity.

Right Other activities can be indicated by the inclusion of tools and equipment. These activity symbols can represent an entire industrial process. Note the use of the outline shape to hold the symbols as a group.

Right Most human activity involves the hand, and hands are a very good basis for symbol designs. Hand gestures or hands with tools are easily suggestive of precise activity.

Right Symbols work best when designed as a group. Disparate designs, picked out of various clip-art sources, will not hold together within the overall design. Use consistent line weights and outline shapes to provide consistency.

Right Where symbols need to be arranged in groups, use careful alignment with even, balanced spacing. Having a consistent shape for a series of symbols makes aligning and spacing much easier.

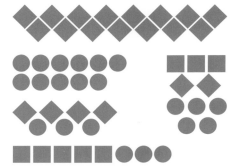

ILLUSTRATIVE DIAGRAMS / SYMBOLS 3

Right The process of creating a symbol from photographic reference requires careful formalization and refinement. Make sure the reference is typical and clear. An underlying grid helps the styling process. An alternative visual treatment is also shown.

28

Right Shearing, or skewing, the symbol, either digitally or in construction, allows interesting views other than flat-on profiles. These views also give a simple 3-D effect.

Left Adding an edge to one or more sides produces another 3-D effect. These are particularly effective in "lifting" the symbol above the page or screen surface. Using software effects such as embossing also creates interesting symbol shapes.

Below Rendering 3-D symbols in tone and color produces full-blown 3-D objects. These images are virtually complete illustrations, rather than simplified icons, yet still reproduce well at small sizes if carefully designed.

Right Symbols can, of course, be created in 3-D form. These have a greater feeling of solidity, even when in simple, line form. Use a standard grid pattern based on 30°, 45°, or 60° angles in order to maintain consistent styling.

Right Symbols can be incorporated in graphics in a number of ways—maybe as a small icon or as a background image. The symbol can even form the basis for the line graph.

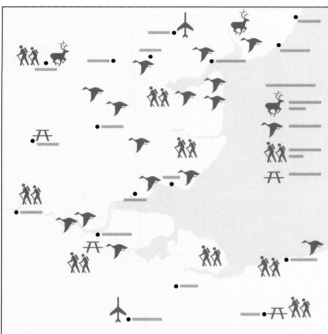

Above Symbols are probably most frequently used in maps, where they function well as a substitute for labels. Here it is essential that each symbol is clearly distinguishable, and that a key explains the function of the icons used.

Right Symbols are also very useful in representing stages in a flow process. In the first of these sports examples, the symbols are basic geometric shapes arranged on a flat plan. Using illustrative icons on an angled view creates a more dynamic image.

ILLUSTRATIVE DIAGRAMS / PICTORIAL I

With so many possible variations in style, structure, and levels of complexity, in this section it is only feasible to deal with the basic guidelines and approach to illustrative pictorial diagrams. As in all methods of diagram design, clarity is the key factor. This begins with a clear brief and carries through with clarity of thought at every stage. The end user does not have direct access to the reference material, so it is the function of the designer/illustrator to extract the fundamental elements from the brief and reassemble them in a clear and pleasing way, free of any ambiguity, clearly labeled where appropriate and without obstructions to understanding. With digital technology, specialized 2-D and 3-D drawing programs, and the vast selection of available clip art covering most subject areas, stunning and functional pictorial diagrams can be generated even by designers with very limited drawing ability.

Right One step up from symbol designs, basic images, such as these simplified human characters and objects, illustrate complex activities in a technical brochure. The clean line and simple use of tone also convey the technological nature of the subject matter.

If you need to include labels on illustrations, make sure they clearly relate to the relevant points. Various methods can be used. Leader lines direct the label to the identified point. The leaders can be at random angles, but look neater when conforming to 90° or 45°. Use a broader, white line as a blanking strip behind leader lines that cross the image. Numbers placed on or against items or located by leader lines allow the labels to be arranged as an easily readable list.

focusing knob   diopter correction
prism casing   eye piece
tripod connector
objective lens

diopter correction   eye piece
focusing knob
prism casing
tripod connector   objective lens

❶ diopter correction
❷ eye piece
❸ focusing knob
❹ objective lens
❺ prism casing
❻ tripod connector

① diopter correction
② eye piece
③ focusing knob
④ objective lens
⑤ prism casing
⑥ tripod connector

Right and below
There are several methods of illustrating elements that would normally be obscured in a straightforward illustration. The cutaway (1) removes pieces of obscuring parts. Ghosting (2) uses transparency to reveal hidden items. The "exploded" illustration (3) separates the various pieces but shows them in relation to their proper position.

Line

Delineated line

Line and tone

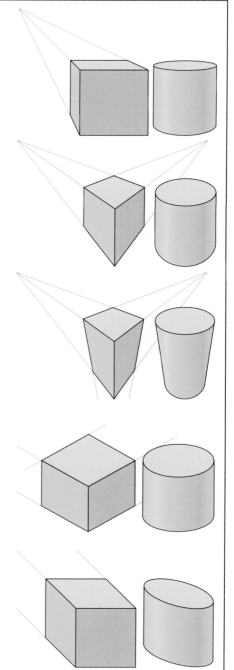

Normally, we view and draw objects in perspective, with parallel edges appearing to converge as they get further away. Lines projected from these edges appear to meet at what we term a vanishing point. A perspective drawing may be based on one, two, or three vanishing points. Diagrams can also be drawn in projections that keep sides parallel. This has the advantage of allowing the edges to be measured and so can make drawing easier. To avoid getting too technical, just two types are shown here—isometric and oblique.
A cube drawn in an isometric projection has vertical sides, and the angles of the faces are at 60° and 120°.
Oblique projections have one plane of the cube drawn face on, and the receding planes angled to one side. Any angle apart from 90° can be used, but 45°, 30°, and 60° are most common.

31

ILLUSTRATIVE DIAGRAMS / PICTORIAL 2

Right A variety of graphic styles can be used for illustrative diagrams. These range from simple black-and-white line, to line and tone, to detailed realistic treatments.

  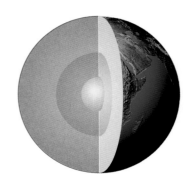

Right Box rules and backgrounds can be useful in giving a regular geometric structure to an otherwise free-form shape. They may be just a basic neutral area of tone or color, or can form part of the illustration.

  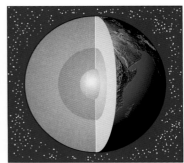

Right There are, of course, many different line styles that can be used in drawing pictorial diagrams. Choose one that suits the subject matter and audience. While a clean, even line suits technical subjects, a varied line is much less formal, perhaps suiting young readers.

Right There is also a wide variety of color treatments from which to select. Again, suit the style to the subject/audience. Also, be consistent in style throughout a publication—unless variety is the style.

Right and below
Illustrative diagrams are often used in sequence, breaking down a complex activity into a series of simple steps. Make sure the steps have enough common elements, so that the series flows visually. Label each stage clearly and make sure that the parts for each are separated well enough, so parts don't get confused. In this example, size remains constant up to stage six, when it is enlarged for clarity. Arrows are used to illustrate movement, and their function is explained in a key. Letters are used to orientate the reader, and these are distinguished from the sequence numbers by color. Note also the subtle use of shading to indicate variations in the planes of surfaces. The sequence is completed by the photograph of the result.

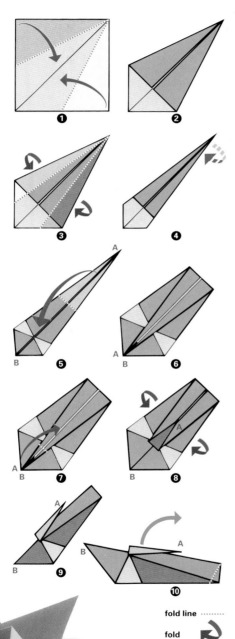

fold line ·······
fold
turn
pull

Right In this diagram, showing how to tie a special knot, color is used to differentiate each strand of the cord. The arrows not only show where the activity of each step takes place, but also indicate how the cord passes over or under itself or the other strand. The apparent lengths of cord are increased as the diagram sequence builds. Horizontal rules separate the steps, and each stage is clearly numbered.

33

ILLUSTRATIVE DIAGRAMS / PICTORIAL 3

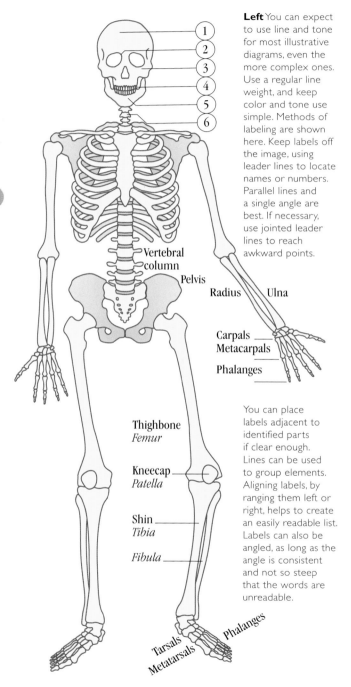

1
2
3
4
5
6

Vertebral
column

Pelvis

Radius   Ulna

Carpals
Metacarpals

Phalanges

Thighbone
Femur

Kneecap
Patella

Shin
Tibia

Fibula

Tarsals   Phalanges
Metatarsals

Left You can expect to use line and tone for most illustrative diagrams, even the more complex ones. Use a regular line weight, and keep color and tone use simple. Methods of labeling are shown here. Keep labels off the image, using leader lines to locate names or numbers. Parallel lines and a single angle are best. If necessary, use jointed leader lines to reach awkward points.

You can place labels adjacent to identified parts if clear enough. Lines can be used to group elements. Aligning labels, by ranging them left or right, helps to create an easily readable list. Labels can also be angled, as long as the angle is consistent and not so steep that the words are unreadable.

Right A diagram like this is relatively simple to construct digitally in line and color. The image is drawn on a 30° projection. It has some basic tone work and graduated tints to give a 3-D effect. Arrows are used to indicate potential movement of parts of the object.

Below Still keeping the detail minimal, and the treatment mostly line and flat tone, this image uses a ghosting technique and arrows to illustrate a simple process. It also is drawn to a regular 30° projection, which makes it simpler to construct using a 2-D vector program.

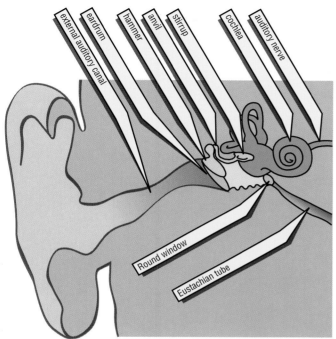

external auditory canal
eardrum
hammer
anvil
stirrup
cochlea
auditory nerve

Round window

Eustachian tube

Left For younger readers, you can give illustrative diagrams a less formal treatment. Here the line weight varies to deliberately soften the style. The angled labels also help to enliven what could otherwise be dry subject matter.

Right Particular care is needed when labeling images with lots of contrasting detail. Place a white line behind the black leader, so the eye can follow the line uninterrupted across the illustration. The angular lines also give visual separation from the image.

1
2
3
4
5
6
7
9
9

35

Left A diagram such as this cross-section through a glacier requires competent drawing skill and good reference. It combines elements created in both vector drawing and raster painting programs.

Above Diagrammatic illustrations of reality are best left to the competent specialists. Despite the wealth of ingenious digital aids now available, it takes years of experience to construct images that are convincing. Nevertheless, the current software does facilitate the rough planning of designs to a surprising degree of finish and can save hours of preplanning time.

Winter wash and pest control on fruit trees

Winter wash and pest control on fruit bushes

Cleaning and sterilizing tools and equipment

Keeping paths and patios clean and disease free

Disease and pest control of flowering plants

Sterilization of plant containers

Moss control on lawns

Cleaning and sterilizing plant supports

Disease and pest control of vegetables

Cleaning and sterilizing frames and cloches

Care of wooden fences and other garden structures

Soil sterilization

Cleaning and sterilizing greenhouses and conservatories

Left This detailed rendering of a traditional brewing oast house would take some time to draw by any method. Creating it with 3-D software gives the designer the flexibility to select the best view for the overall design. It also enables variations of lighting effect to be tried. The image could be incorporated into an animated sequence, and could have the further advantage of being available for reuse (subject to copyright conditions).

Left Except for the cut-out shape and the labeling, this diagram is a conventional illustration. This kind of realism would be difficult to create with a 3-D program; and for a sensitive rendering, competent illustrative skills would certainly be required.

Right You may need to create illustrations for cover designs or as more decorative images. An informal assembly of pictorial symbols such as this represents technical subject matter well and is simple to create.

37

STATISTICAL DIAGRAMS / TABLES I

Presenting data in a clear and unambiguous way is the function of the information designer. Even when data is displayed in tabular form, as a matrix of values, careful planning and preparation is necessary. The eyes of the user need to be guided directly to the salient information, without the interruption of graphic clutter or unplanned confusion.

There are many graphic tools at the designer's disposal, and intelligent application of these will create tables that are easy to read and therefore clear to understand. As in all information design, consistency of treatment is no less vital than diligent planning.

Tables will, of course, often include text as well as data, while others will contain only text. In order to enhance the appearance and usability of a table, you can incorporate basic graphics, such as small icons or even simple charts.

Right In its simplest form, a table is just a list of information presented in an ordered fashion. This requires the careful alignment of table entries and can be helped by the inclusion of horizontal and/or vertical rules.

Right This basic table sets out the data so that all the vertical columns are equal in size, as are the horizontal rows. The column headings are centered above the relevant entries and are separated from the body of the table by a rule. Value totals are set in bold.

Right Column widths can be varied to fit wide headings or text entries. To carry the eye across the table, "fill characters" can be used instead of rules; they also prevent the eye being drawn down by a vertical line of repeating entries, such as zeros.

Right Horizontal and/or vertical rules help structure the table. Use rules when tables need to be wide or deep. They help guide the user. Keep the rules as subtle as possible, and leave enough space around each entry.

Right Alignment of type in tables is a matter of style and common sense. Text often looks better centered, while row headings might be better arranged flush left or right. Decimal points and commas for thousands and millions should be vertically aligned.

	thousands	decimal
	0,000	0.0
	00,000	00.0
	000,000	000.0
	00,000	00.0
	00,000	00.0
	000,000	000.0
	0,000	0.0
	00,000	00.0
	000,000	000.0
	0,000	0.0
	00,000	00.0

Right Instead of rules, bands of tints alternating with white bands can be used behind rows of entries as a means of directing the eye across the horizontal lines of data. Keep the tints subtle, so they don't interfere with the visibility of the entries.

Right Alternating bands of color can also be effective, as long as you don't make them too prominent. If color is not an option, try two gray values. Or use a constant tint of gray or color behind the whole table, with white rules as separators.

Right Effects such as embossing, engraving, or even subtle bas relief can work well as horizontal dividers. But bear in mind that what you're trying to do is to facilitate the reading of the table as a whole. Don't let the effects impede.

Right Vertical tint bands and rules also help with visibility and assimilation of data. Again, keep tints subtle—otherwise, what should be a background aid will become a foreground nuisance.

Right Embossing and engraving effects can work just as well on columns as on rows. But it may be better to use the fancier treatment for one direction only, combined with a simple rule technique for the other.

Right As column widths are likely to be greater than row heights, some subtle effects—such as a drop shadow or a curved or chamfered edge—can be very effective in giving tables a little extra style treatment.

39

STATISTICAL DIAGRAMS / TABLES 2

Right When designing tables, you need to take a look at the way entries are ordered. Often they are in an arbitrary sequence, a result of the data compilation, which will not aid the user. Always refer to the client before changing the order.

Belgium	Europe	10.87	54.65	65.52
Estonia	Europe	16.98	68.35	85.33
South Africa	Africa	20.35	34.55	54.90
USA	North America	13.68	29.47	43.15
Mexico	Central America	17.25	45.36	62.61
China	Asia	12.84	75.11	87.95
Australia	Oceania	11.65	36.24	47.89
UK	Europe	9.48	62.87	72.35
Peru	South America	14.32	21.65	35.97
Pakistan	Asia	8.97	63.47	72.44
Kenya	Africa	17.33	47.11	64.44
Germany	Europe	19.56	33.68	53.24

Right More complex table layouts will have subsections or even sub-subsets. Careful typographical layout will help the reader to see these in their correct relationship. Indenting the subsets is effective, but takes up horizontal space.

Right Tables supplied in a spreadsheet or similar format can be adjusted easily using available tools. It is worth learning some spreadsheet basics for this. The whole of the table can be reordered so that row headings are in alphabetical order.

Australia	Oceania	11.65	36.24	47.89
Belgium	Europe	10.87	54.65	65.52
China	Asia	12.84	75.11	87.95
Estonia	Europe	16.98	68.35	85.33
Germany	Europe	19.56	33.68	53.24
Kenya	Africa	17.33	47.11	64.44
Mexico	Central America	17.25	45.36	62.61
Pakistan	Asia	8.97	63.47	72.44
Peru	South America	14.32	21.65	35.97
South Africa	Africa	20.35	34.55	54.90
UK	Europe	9.48	62.87	72.35
USA	North America	13.68	29.47	43.15

Right Varying the weights of rules is useful if horizontal space is tight. Make sure the difference in weight is apparent, without making the rules too bold or incongruous.

Right Perhaps one column of data is more important than the others. The table could then be set so that this column ranks entries in ascending or descending order.

South Africa	Africa	20.35	34.55	54.90
Kenya	Africa	17.33	47.11	64.44
China	Asia	12.84	75.11	87.95
Pakistan	Asia	8.97	63.47	72.44
Mexico	Central America	17.25	45.36	62.61
Germany	Europe	19.56	33.68	53.24
Estonia	Europe	16.98	68.35	85.33
Belgium	Europe	10.87	54.65	65.52
UK	Europe	9.48	62.87	72.35
USA	North America	13.68	29.47	43.15
Australia	Oceania	11.65	36.24	47.89
Peru	South America	14.32	21.65	35.97

Right If color bands are used, subsets can be related by having tints of main colors. Make sure your tint values are enough to be distinguishable, but not so strong that they generate an unpleasant or garish effect.

Right It may be that the final column, the totals or summary, contains the most significant facts. So perhaps this column should determine the ordering of the others.

China	Asia	12.84	75.11	87.95
Estonia	Europe	16.98	68.35	85.33
Pakistan	Asia	8.97	63.47	72.44
UK	Europe	9.48	62.87	72.35
Belgium	Europe	10.87	54.65	65.52
Kenya	Africa	17.33	47.11	64.44
Mexico	Central America	17.25	45.36	62.61
South Africa	Africa	20.35	34.55	54.9
Germany	Europe	19.56	33.68	53.24
Australia	Oceania	11.65	36.24	47.89
USA	North America	13.68	29.47	43.15
Peru	South America	14.32	21.65	35.97

Right Bolder and lighter type variations or the use of capitals are often enough to distinguish subsets, but fancier effects such as row bands with reversed-out type or a drop shadow can be used to highlight headings.

Right Column heads may also have subsets. Here, again, careful typographic arrangement will make relationships clear and easily understandable. This arrangement will require adequate space allocation.

Right This method employs tint bands in the vertical columns in order to group subsections. Tints can be kept simple, or you might be able to use subtle treatments to indicate hierarchical levels of subsets.

Right If horizontal space is limited, fitting long labels is always a problem. Angled headings are easier to read than vertical type. Allow enough space at the end to fit an angled rule, remembering that its length is determined by the longest entry.

Right Angled heads are also useful when column entries are particularly narrow or in nondata/text tables. The angled column heading fits the narrow measure comfortably and is readable even at quite steep angles.

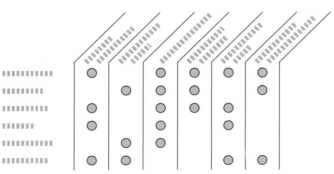

STATISTICAL DIAGRAMS / TABLES 3

Right Tables that are mostly or entirely text-based will need variable row and column dimensions. Work these to a grid structure so that depths are based on one, two, or three lines, etc. The column widths should be determined by the longest entry in each.

Right A table with a variety of entries (for example, text, data, and symbols) needs special care in entry alignment. Hanging all row entries from the uppermost line is better than centering vertically.

Right Negative values frequently occur in data tables. These can be identified by a minus sign, but if you need to highlight them there are several methods. A simple typographic treatment, familiar to accountants, puts the value in brackets. More noticeable is a variation in weight of type used for negatives, so long as it is visibly different. Use color for even greater emphasis. Alternatively, the cell containing the value can be emphasized by graphic treatment.

	12.3	400	(-23.0)
	(-1.3)	550	25.6
	8.9	231	(-54.5)
	7.3	954	62.3
	3.5	621	(-44.3)
	(-4.5)	333	(-33.7)

	12.3	400	**-23.0**
	-1.3	550	25.6
	8.9	231	**-54.5**
	7.3	954	62.3
	3.5	621	**-44.3**
	-4.5	333	**-33.7**

	12.3	400	-23.0
	-1.3	550	25.6
	8.9	231	-54.5
	7.3	954	62.3
	3.5	621	-44.3
	-4.5	333	-33.7

Right There are times when you may need to emphasize other variations in values, particularly in larger tables. Here the use of type weights (so long as the difference is not too subtle), colored type, or graphically differentiated cells will be helpful.

Right Add emphasis to selected points in a table by simulating a "highlighter" effect, a hand-drawn ring, or an underscore.

	300	300	300
	950	950	**950**
	298	298	298
	230	230	230
	254	254	254
	265	265	265
	274	274	274
	269	269	269
	264	264	264

	102	102	102
	274	274	274
	365	365	365
	854	854	854
	1006	1006	1006
	874	874	874
	354	354	354
	655	655	655
	574	574	574

Right Where you need to show only a limited range of conditions in a table format, use simple icons with an explanatory key. This will help keep the chart compact and will also give it visual appeal.

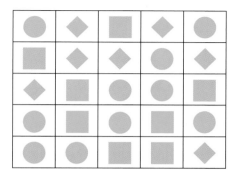

Right Extend the range of possible conditions by varying the size and/or color of icons. You can also make some of them solid fills and some of them outlines. But don't make so many variations that the user has to struggle to interpret the table.

Right A wide range of graphics can be employed as icons in tables. Using 3-D symbols (such as map pins or shadows) and well-produced pictograms (even flags) will liven up an otherwise staid table.

Right Values can be shown in a table format by using multiple or repeating icons. Plan the chart carefully, allowing enough room for the highest value entry and for any text that needs to be included.

Right You can also illustrate values in a table by incorporating a simple bar behind the data in the cell. As the maximum bar length is restricted, subtle differences will not show well.

Right Other types of information graphics can be combined in the table, too. This example shows simple graph and pie charts being used quite effectively, despite their relatively tiny size.

STATISTICAL DIAGRAMS / LINE GRAPHS I

Line graphs are widely used to represent data in graphic form. Essentially, they are sequential points of value plotted on a grid matrix with some form of line between the points. The line indicates the rate of change or difference along the progression of the chart: the steeper the line, the greater the rate of change. Line graphs are easy to produce and commonly used, and can be very dull. But a few simple graphic techniques, applied with intelligence and design sensitivity, can make them very effective communication vehicles.

Keep in mind that the function of the graph is to show the rate of change between points. This is important, because the angle of the line will be varied by the format of the chart—a narrow chart will emphasize the gradient, whereas a wide chart will lessen the effect.

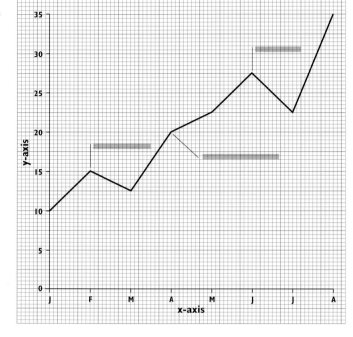

Right A simple line chart with the basic elements identified.

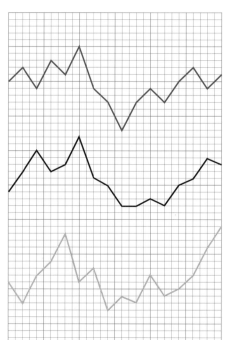

Left Several lines may be incorporated on the same grid. These may be conveniently separate, but if they cross over you must make sure they are quite distinct and won't be confused by the user.

Right Two or more lines may be combined in a single chart but plotted so they accumulate in value. In a graph like this, it must be made clear that the lower line is a subdivision of the total value shown by the top line.

Right Filling in the area between the graph's plot line and the base gives the chart more weight. To emphasize the effect, in this example only the horizontal grid lines have been shown, and these are treated differently above and below the plot line.

44

Above These examples show how the angles between points on the plot line are affected by varying the width of the graph—by either compressing or expanding the x-axis while keeping the same depth.

Right Line graphs don't have to be plotted horizontally, although that is the convention. Turning the chart 90° creates an interesting variation. It also lets you achieve even more dramatic angles on the plot line.

Left As an alternative to plotting two sets of data on one graph, you can plot two charts mirrored so that the base line forms a central axis. This "butterfly" chart is particularly useful if the two data sets are so close that the lines would be confused if on the same grid.

Left The inverse butterfly chart "splits" the central axis by placing it on the left and right sides, and plots the graphs so that they "point" to the center. Use a tint fill to make absolutely clear where the body of the graph is.

Below Some data, such as an area's typical temperature over a year, forms a cyclical pattern. This works best as a circular graph—the

x-axis forming the circle and the y-axis radiating from the center. As well as making an interesting shape, it shows the repeat process.

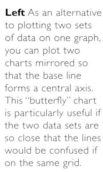

STATISTICAL DIAGRAMS / LINE GRAPHS 2

Right When choosing a suitable line weight for a graph, keep in mind that digitally produced thick lines generate extended mitres, particularly on acute angles, and these may confuse readers. Limit mitre extents with software controls.

Right Point markers can be used to give emphasis to the data points. They can also be used to differentiate lines, as long as there aren't too many lines on the graph.

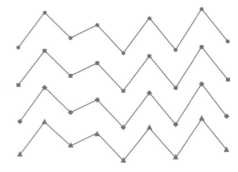

46

Right In addition to line thickness, line style can be varied in order to differentiate multiple lines on monochrome graphs. Make sure the variations in line style are clearly apparent, particularly if the lines are clustered or cross each other frequently. Even when color is available, you may have to vary the style of the lines so that they are clearly distinguished.

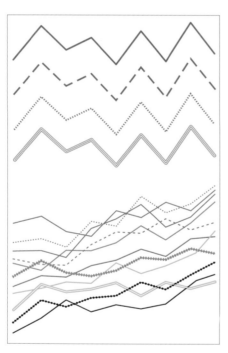

Right Some specialized data sets include high and low or maximum, median, and minimum values. On a single line graph, you can use a band to show the range, or insert markers at the data points.

Right This variation on an ordinary line graph has a change in condition at various time points of each data set. This is shown by the change in line treatment. Use a key to explain the reason for the change.

Right Graph styles can be varied by the treatment of the underlying grid. You can either show the grid in full or show just the x-axis and y-axis. Provided that the data points are labeled or easily read, the grid can be left out and the scales shown by tick marks.

Right You can make negative values on graphs more apparent by coloring the grid area below the zero base on the *y*-axis. Alternatively, color the part of the plot area that dips below the line, or change the color of the plot line for the negative part.

Right Sometimes you may have to combine two lines that are plotted to different axis values. Show the axes on opposite sides of the graph, and use color to relate the line to its axis. It will also help if the axis labels have the same color.

Right Percentage graphs plot values as a proportion of one hundred, with either side of the plot line having a value. Make this clear by using colors of equal visual weight for both sides. This type of graph often works well if turned 90°.

Right When one value in a data set varies greatly from all the others, plotting all the points on the same scale will limit differentiation for all but the anomalous value. Various graphic techniques allow you to show all the points without minimizing the close values.

Right In order to exaggerate rates of change, you may want to use a base for the graph that is higher than zero. There are several ways to make this clear to the user. You can leave out the base line of the grid, or use one of these more graphic techniques.

STATISTICAL DIAGRAMS / LINE GRAPHS 3

Right Identifying lines on multiple graphs can be problematic, especially where lines are close together and overlapping. You might have space close enough to each line to label it—but you'll probably need to use various angles, and the result can be messy and unclear.

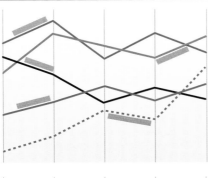

Provided that the line styles are clearly distinguishable (which they should be), use a key listing to identify them. Place the key in a clear area of the graph, so it doesn't hide any plot lines. Or make the graph narrower and place the key to the side.

Making the graph a bit narrower allows space at the end (or beginning) of lines where they can be named, so long as they are sufficiently separated at the first or last plot point.

If the lines are too tightly clustered to accommodate adjacent labels, you can use leaders to locate the relevant lines. Otherwise, resort to the key method described above.

Right Whether or not a grid is used, you may want to show the actual values of data points. Position labels so they don't interfere with the plot line. Angling the labels can help. Or use leader lines, so that the values can appear as a row of data.

Right If space and style permit, you can have point markers big enough to contain the data labels. An alternative is to use arrow devices that are separate from the line, placed to follow the rise and fall of the plot pattern.

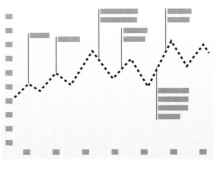

Right and below Key events that have influenced the data on a chart may need to be labeled. The type matter is likely to vary in length and appear at relatively arbitrary points. Use leader lines to locate them. A horizontal plot allows the events to be listed.

Right Using 3-D effects on line graphs gives a chart a lot of punch. But be careful not to lose or distort the data. The plot line appears to float with a soft shadow, but make sure it relates visually to the grid. These other 3-D plot lines also need careful attention.

Right You can apply 3-D treatment to filled graphs, creating a solid block appearance. Here again, make sure any grid lines clearly relate to the plot. The third sample keeps the block very shallow but uses shadow to lift the plot area.

Right Multiple graphs can be placed one behind the other, so long as the plot lines of each graph are visible above the one in front. Make the grid offset alignment clear, too. Here it has been shown only on the face of each plot area.

Right Butterfly graphs can also be drawn in 3-D. In order to treat both charts evenly, in this example the view appears to be from above. A view offset to one side would give emphasis to one or the other of the graphs.

Right This unusual view and orientation presents the chart as if seen from below or head on. It is very effective in emphasizing the plot line.

STATISTICAL DIAGRAMS / LINE GRAPHS 4

Right A little creativity can transform even staid graphics. This series of charts could have been plotted as one long, ordinary graph. Breaking it up into five-year segments and making a feature of this creates a more interesting effect.

50

Right These three graphic devices also help to liven up what could otherwise be dull charts, and all are relatively easy digital effects. The first gives the semblance of pins joined by string. An engraved effect is used in the second, and the third employs shooting stars.

Right Incorporating pictorial elements in a chart can be eye-catching. But too often it is badly done, with the plot line all but obscured. Keep the pictures subtle, and use color and tone to make the plot area clearly distinguishable from the grid.

Right Imaginative use of chart combinations can create interesting effects. Plotting the lower chart so that it resembles a shadow cast by the 3-D graphs works well when the data for the vertical charts is more closely related than the data for the base chart.

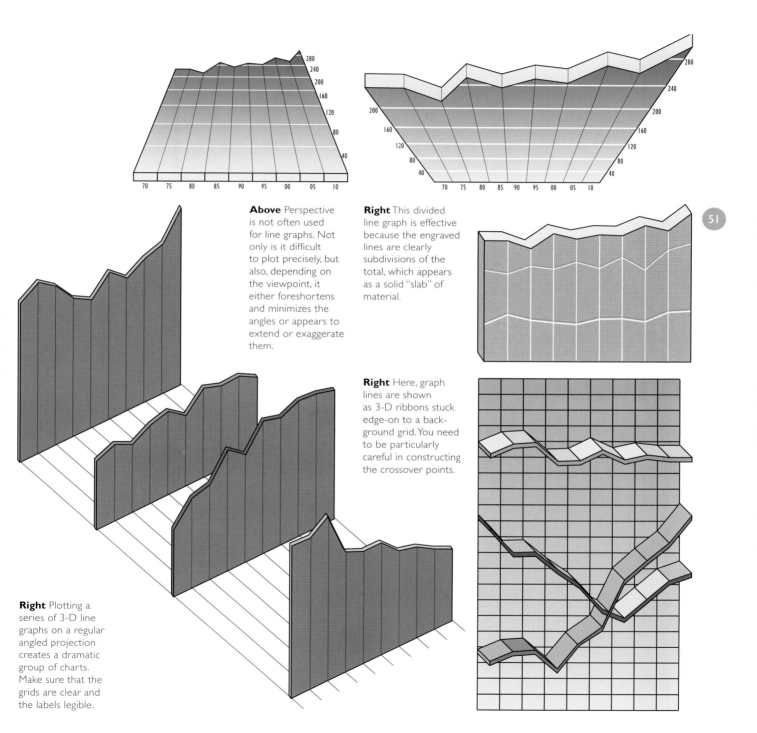

Above Perspective is not often used for line graphs. Not only is it difficult to plot precisely, but also, depending on the viewpoint, it either foreshortens and minimizes the angles or appears to extend or exaggerate them.

Right This divided line graph is effective because the engraved lines are clearly subdivisions of the total, which appears as a solid "slab" of material.

Right Here, graph lines are shown as 3-D ribbons stuck edge-on to a background grid. You need to be particularly careful in constructing the crossover points.

Right Plotting a series of 3-D line graphs on a regular angled projection creates a dramatic group of charts. Make sure that the grids are clear and the labels legible.

51

STATISTICAL DIAGRAMS / SCATTER GRAPHS

Scatter graphs are a rather specialized type of chart, most often used in scientific and statistical analysis. Like line graphs, scatter graphs are plotted on a grid consisting of an *x*-axis and a *y*-axis—but, whereas line graphs show a progression of points and the rate of change between them, a scatter graph has individual points. The significance is the relationship of each point to all the others on the chart. Configurations of points may illustrate a trend, which can appear as a line.

Right This shows the underlying structure of the scatter graph. Points are located by the intersection of two values, one on the *x*-axis and one on the *y*-axis. The axes will usually show two data variables, rather than a chronological sequence along one axis only.

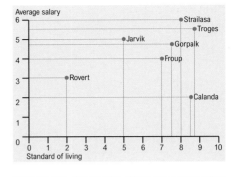

Right Points on scatter graphs are marked by a suitable device—a small circle or square, for example—which can be in color. Where two or more sets of data are combined in one chart, each group's points need to be distinguishable.

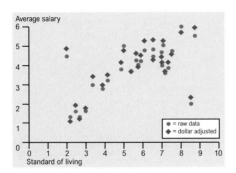

Right A basic scatter graph is simply a configuration of points, often with groups or clusters. If the graph is indicating a general pattern, it may not be necessary to label any of the points.

Right When point labels are required, care and patience is needed, particularly when dealing with clusters. Leader lines can be used to locate points. Angled type may be helpful if the configuration permits.

Right This variation of the scatter graph is divided into labeled quadrants. These give a general analysis of the conditions pertaining to the points that fall within them. It is best to keep the divisions subtle.

Right It might be even better to use leader lines for all the points, keeping the labels well away from them. Alternatively, a number system should take up less space and can be used across a series of diagrams.

Right Various graphic techniques can be used to enliven scatter graphs. These include 3-D effects such as embossing and drop shadowing, and even more elaborate treatments —such as map pins, pyramids, or cylinders.

Right Trend lines can be either dominant or subtle, depending on editorial and design preference. In some cases, data for a broad band may be supplied.

Right A third element of data can be incorporated in a scatter graph by giving the area of the point marker a value. In this case, the color of the point marker changes according to a keyed scale of values.

over 50% funded
40–49%
30–39%
20–29%
under 20%

Below Another way to display a third value is shown in this 3-D variation of the scatter graph. Here the third value is plotted along a vertical z-axis.

Tokyo
Madrid
Seattle
Moscow
Seoul
London
Boston
Rome
New York
Berlin
Brussels
Paris

STATISTICAL DIAGRAMS / BAR CHARTS 1

Bar charts are probably the most frequently used form of data graphics. Essentially, the bar chart represents values as measurable lengths (the width of the bars remains constant). By placing two or more bars side by side you can see the absolute values of the bars and the relative difference between them. You can draw bar charts vertically—sometimes called column charts—or horizontally. They can of course be drawn at any angle you like, though in order to be read successfully all the bars should extend from a recognizable baseline, so that the bar lengths are easily compared.

The bars are usually labeled individually, although a grid or other scaling method can be used. You can plot the bars against a regular scale or a logarithmic one, or they can be drawn in perspective. However, perspective effects do distort and may make the charts hard to read accurately. Bar charts can be enhanced by using 3-D and other effects.

Right In the most basic bar charts, bars of equal width are placed along one axis. Bars can abut or be evenly spaced. The quantity or value is shown by the length of the bar. Typically, each bar shows the amount of something at a different point in time (an annual value, for example); or the bars may show how individual items compare over a given period of time. Labels are usually included to identify bars and for values, although it is possible to use a scale or grid instead of value labels.

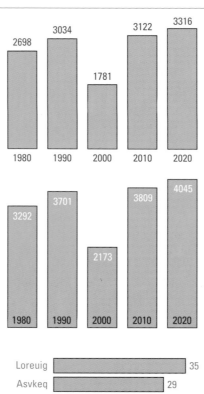

Right Charts can be plotted horizontally instead of vertically, so that the bar values are on the x-axis and the incidence of bars is along the y-axis.

Loreuig 35
Asvkeq 29
Lntqnxt 33
Xoreuts 11
Ghinjacx 26
Nywig 32
Mlskcef 17
Lishvd 33

Right Labels can be put wherever you like, so long as they relate to their bar clearly and you treat them all the same way. You can place all the labels inside the bars, or all outside, or do both. In some instances you might want to vary this: for example, you might want to place labels outside short bars, even though other bars have their labels inside. In each case, leave enough space between the label and the edge of the bar. Long labels can be angled, but keep the angle consistent and make sure the label is readable.

Right A numbered or color-coded key helps when labels are bigger than bar widths. Place the key in any convenient area of the chart. In a series of charts, be consistent about the position of the key.

Right The width of the bars is a matter of style and common sense. Narrow bars may be necessary if many bars are to be included in restricted space. Broad bars give visual weight.

Left If data doesn't have a set sequence, you can arrange bars according to some other criterion, as in these three examples. This could be alphabetical order (*top*), or in order of increasing (*center*) or decreasing (*bottom*) values.

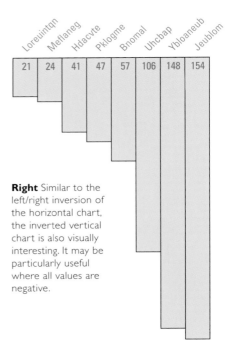

55

Below Although horizontal bar charts are usually aligned left, transposing the chart can produce interesting effects. Aligning the chart right also allows you to range the bars' identity labels tidily left, against the ends of the bars.

Right Similar to the left/right inversion of the horizontal chart, the inverted vertical chart is also visually interesting. It may be particularly useful where all values are negative.

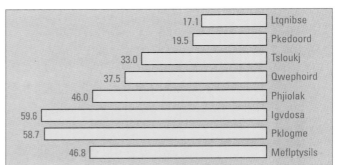

STATISTICAL DIAGRAMS / BAR CHARTS 2

Right Bars don't have to be bars. Any linear structure that has a measurable length can be used—but make sure the style you choose suits the intended readership. For example, a stylized pattern might not be suitable for children.

Right You can make bar charts using type characters—either from a regular type font or from dingbats. It's therefore possible to produce charts in a word-processing or page-layout program.

Right Constructing bars from pictograms adds interest. It's best to have the number of symbols relate to the value. Make each symbol represent one hundred or one thousand items, for example.

Right Creating fractions of symbols, in order to have them relate closely to the actual value, is simple with a rectangular shape. But with a freer outline (such as the motorcycle) you have to exaggerate the smaller fractions, making sure each segment is distinct.

Right Thousands of symbols are available as clip art, but be sure to match styles. Use common sense in the selection (e.g., let derricks relate to oil production, barrels to consumption). Make use of color to distinguish similar icons that represent different subjects.

Left Some subjects lend themselves to symbolism; distance traveled, for example, with combined aircraft and vapor trail or car and road. But beware of misleading analogies: here, for example, railroad cars suggest numbers of passengers carried, not travel distance.

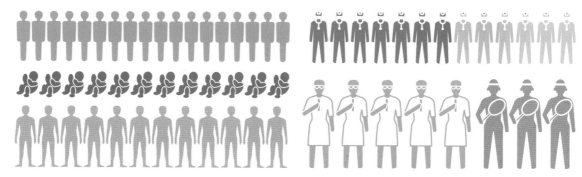

Right Charts very often relate to human activity, and lines of human figures are a good way to liven up data presentation. See the symbols section on pages 24–29 for guidance on creating suitable pictograms.

Left If you need to produce a more visible bar form, try combining stronger graphic elements with smaller pictograms.

Right This illustrates a common error in charts using human figures. The icons vary in size, and the height represents the value. But the eye sees the overall proportion, which is misleading. For comparison, look at the stacked rows of figures showing the same values.

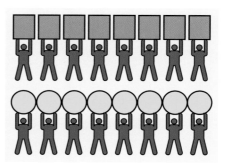

Right Some subject matter inspires an icon that contains the chart, rather than the other way around. Here the content of each test tube shows the value.

Left A flag on a flagpole presents an identifiable object that can be adjusted easily to show a height value. This is obviously useful for charts comparing states or countries, but the flags could bear company logos or any pictogram.

Right Chocolate consumption and similar subjects lend themselves readily to graphic portrayal. Use your imagination to create eye-catching charts.

Switzerland
Britain
Norway
Austria
Germany
Belgium
Denmark
Ireland
Sweden
Holland
Australia
France
Italy

STATISTICAL DIAGRAMS / BAR CHARTS 3

Right You can draw grids for bar charts instead of or as a supplement to value labels. The grid helps the user measure the bars and differences in bar height. Either draw the grid across the chart's full width (or depth), or just behind bars, or only on the bar front.

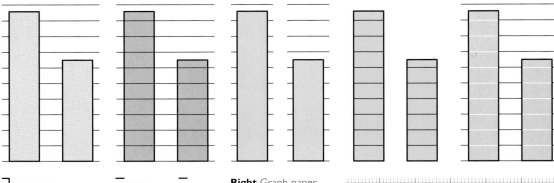

Right Instead of a full grid, you may prefer a simple scale alongside the chart, like a ruler, to measure the bars.

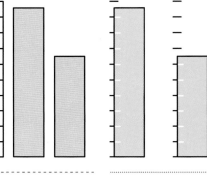

Right Graph paper can make a subtle but effective grid for bar diagrams. Obviously, you should make sure that the graph grid relates to the values of the bars. And it may be too restrictive for a series of charts where you need the flexibility to vary the grid measure.

Right Line styles for grids are a matter of taste—or house style. The lines can be solid or broken, and any legible color. If there are subdivisions on the grid, vary the line weight. Be inventive, while making sure that the grid remains functional.

Right Here are some more variations on grid style. Graduated tones or color tints can emphasize value differences, with the contrast increasing for the higher bars. A dot structure subtly implies the underlying grid. Also subtle is a pencil effect, with the bar as hard line.

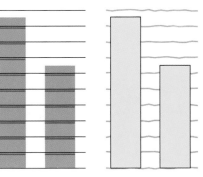

Right Used in more specialized charts, the logarithmic scale helps when there are great differences between values. Logarithmic scales never start from zero. There are several versions of the scale, but base ten is the most frequently used.

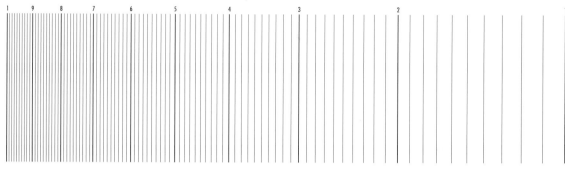

Right Perspective scales can start from zero, but plotting bar size accurately is virtually impossible. The structure is based on diagonal lines intersecting at the halfway point. In perspective, the same rule applies.

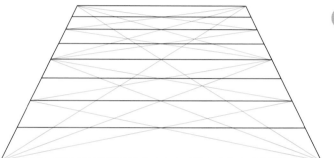

Right and below In some charts it may be necessary to draw the grid to a fixed value—for example, charts based on a 100% total. In other cases a "benchmark" value may need to be shown. This may vary for each bar in the chart.

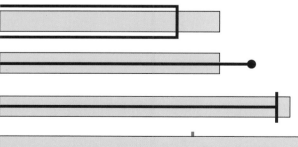

Right Grids often can be incorporated in the structure of the bars. Divide the bar so that each segment equals a scale unit. The final segment may need to be "cut" to show a fraction. By representing known quantities, pictograms can also be used as grid units.

STATISTICAL DIAGRAMS / BAR CHARTS 4

Right Using 3-D effects can make bar charts much more appealing. But if they are overdone, they can be misleading and/or ugly. Often, a simple offset shadow is enough. This and other basic effects (all of them relatively easy to achieve) are shown here.

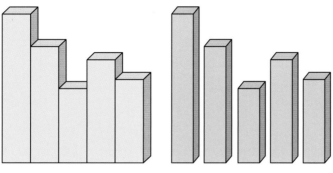

Right This unusual variation of the shadow effect shows the bar appearing to be cut out of the plane of the grid.

Right Adding a top and side to bars gives them solidity—but don't overdo it. These enhancements are decorative, and it is the face of the bar that carries the real information. Lines all follow the same angle of projection, which should be consistent for a series of charts.

Right Plotting bars with a shallow depth on an oblique or isometric projection makes them appear sideways to the reader. Nevertheless, the bars accurately represent the values in the data.

Right Oblique or isometric projections are useful for creating 3-D bars. Angles are constant, and you can either draw the bars on a horizontal base or plot them along the angle of projection to create a more interesting array.

Right Aligning horizontal bars along a central vertical axis creates a pyramid effect. You can keep the angles of the bar ends consistent or draw them to a single vanishing point.

Left You can achieve another simple 3-D effect by adding an elliptical or circular top and bottom to the bars. The resulting cylinder effect can be enhanced by some subtle shading, or by adding more ellipses at measured intervals along the bar.

Right You can also plot cylindrical bars along angled axes.

Right There are many simple shapes that can be used to create interesting 3-D bars. Just make sure that the visual effect does not interfere with the integrity of the chart.

Right Be careful when combining a grid with a 3-D effect. Don't make it hard for the reader to relate the grid to the bar. Wrap the grid around the bar or have it clearly behind. Keeping the bars "shallow" helps. Or just have the grid on the bar alone.

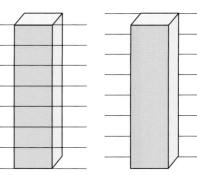

Right Because of its association with the conventional plotting of charts, graph paper makes an effective background. Here it has been combined with another traditional plotting artifact—the map pin.

Right Of course, you can create 3-D bars by drawing a series of objects in 3-D. Shading also can be used to enhance the visual effect.

STATISTICAL DIAGRAMS / BAR CHARTS 5

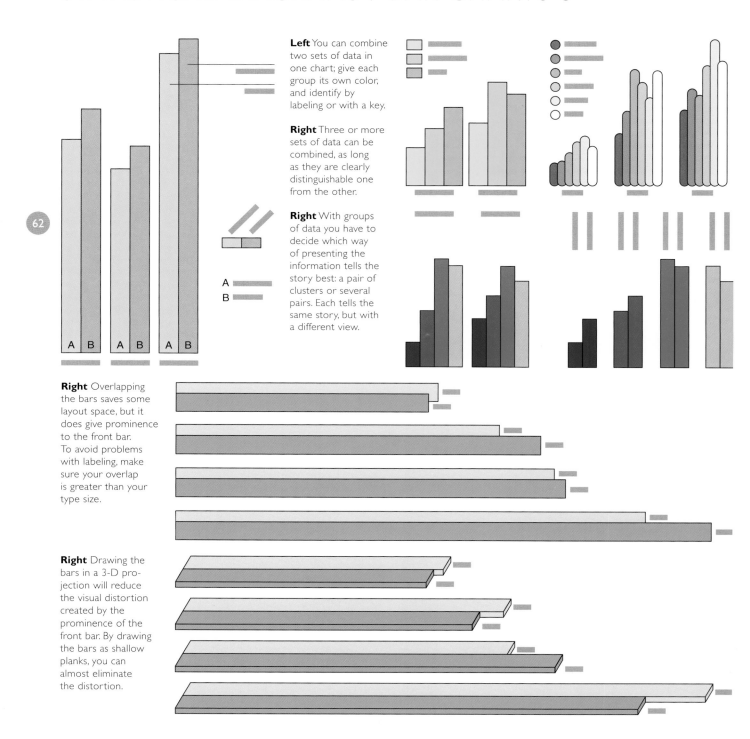

Left You can combine two sets of data in one chart; give each group its own color, and identify by labeling or with a key.

Right Three or more sets of data can be combined, as long as they are clearly distinguishable one from the other.

Right With groups of data you have to decide which way of presenting the information tells the story best: a pair of clusters or several pairs. Each tells the same story, but with a different view.

Right Overlapping the bars saves some layout space, but it does give prominence to the front bar. To avoid problems with labeling, make sure your overlap is greater than your type size.

Right Drawing the bars in a 3-D projection will reduce the visual distortion created by the prominence of the front bar. By drawing the bars as shallow planks, you can almost eliminate the distortion.

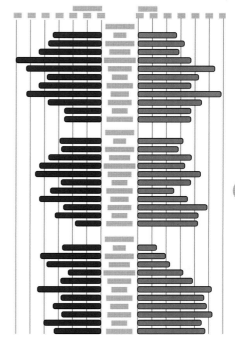

Left Pairs of bars can work well as mirror charts where bars are placed on either side of a baseline wide enough to include labels.

Right Using a grid to show the values, you can combine several of these charts in a relatively tight space.

Left This variation on the mirror chart allows more room for labeling—provided the pattern of data suits the arrangement. If need be, you can move the bar indent labels to the left or right side of the chart.

Left, below left, and right Drawing mirror bar charts at symmetrical angles introduces a dynamic appearance. You will have to be careful about fitting labels on or around the bars.

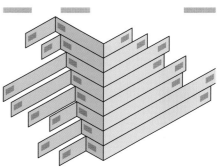

Right This concertina bar diagram combines three charts in an intriguing design solution. The central chart is arranged in order of decreasing values to allow the bars of the left-hand chart to be seen clearly.

Left and right If you have data for a bar chart showing a total value and breakdown of composite parts, you can produce a stacked or split bar chart. This simply places the component bars end to end, either as a vertical column chart or horizontal bar graph.

Left Because of the structure, you can plot lines between separated split bars to show rate of change, much as a line graph does.

Right and above Split bar charts work well in 3-D. Use a color key to identify the parts. Even if you have only one set of data, you can present this as a split or stacked bar, rather than as a regular bar chart.

Left and right Fitting labels to a split (stacked, composite, or divided) bar chart can present problems. Use leader lines to locate labels to parts. Drawing the chart in 3-D and separating the composite parts works well, so long as you make sure the amount of separation is enough to fit in the label. Offsetting the segments also helps to accommodate data labels—as shown here in the stepped split bar chart.

Left and right
Angling 3-D stacked bars creates interest. In particular, the mirrored stacked-bar chart appearing to project from the page surface gives a very dramatic effect.

Left and right If you use pictograms as the basic bar structure, make sure the shape is as even as possible to avoid giving undue prominence to any part. The distortion of the base of the test-tube (*right*) is less misleading than the uneven areas of the human symbol (*left*).

Right When the opportunity arises, make use of pictorial enhancements, such as the flags identifying the countries that feature in this chart. The flagpoles become the split bars, and thus an exciting graphic effect is created in a very simple way.

Right This powerful chart is produced by combining two split bar charts on one base cylinder. The total value for each side is equal, being 100%. The chart works well because its component parts are similar in size, so labeling is simplified. It also succeeds in creating a dramatic image out of relatively undramatic data.

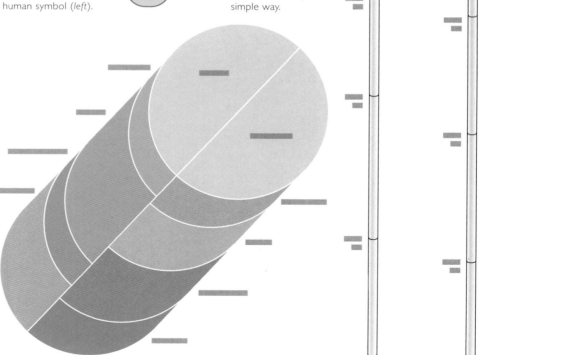

STATISTICAL DIAGRAMS / BAR CHARTS 7

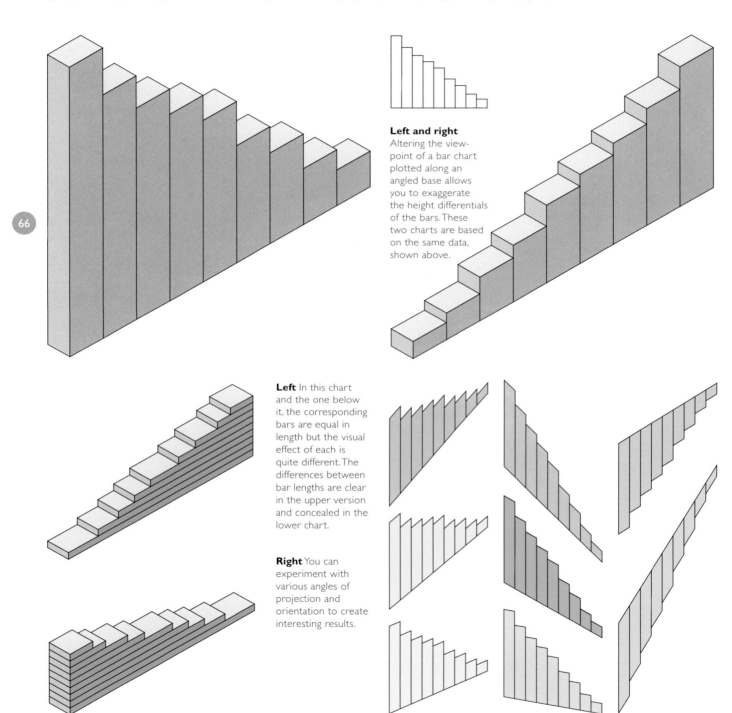

Left and right
Altering the viewpoint of a bar chart plotted along an angled base allows you to exaggerate the height differentials of the bars. These two charts are based on the same data, shown above.

Left In this chart and the one below it, the corresponding bars are equal in length but the visual effect of each is quite different. The differences between bar lengths are clear in the upper version and concealed in the lower chart.

Right You can experiment with various angles of projection and orientation to create interesting results.

Left and right
Use perspective to exaggerate or reduce the differences in bar lengths. These two chart examples are drawn from the same data on a one-point perspective projection, but the version on the left has a much more dramatic presence.

Right Even one-point perspective makes it possible to produce powerful, dynamic bar charts.

Left Three-point perspective projections create even more dramatic effects, and are relatively easy to produce with 3-D software.

300m   260m   210m   160m   120m   90m   40m

Left and right
You can use curved or circular baselines to produce interesting results. The curved base can be used effectively to fit charts into tight spaces while keeping bar lengths at a maximum.

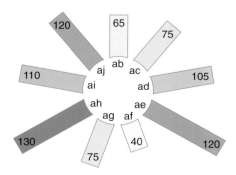

120   65   75
110   aj ab ac   105
  ai ad
  ah ag af ae
130   75   40   120

BAR CHARTS 8

Right Sometimes charts need to include one or two values that are much greater than all the others. There are several ways of drawing the chart with the excessive bar extending off, while maintaining the visual differentiation of the remaining bars.

Right If you want to show the complete bar in the chart, you can plot a spiral bar. Construct the long bar to fit the required shape, then draw and duplicate small circles to the bar width. Fit these along the bar length to calculate proportional sizes for the other bars.

Right Similar to the spiral, but much easier to construct, this bar diagram uses curves to highlight the difference in values. Use it when values are not too dissimilar but space for the chart is tight. A grid of equal-sized circles aids accurate plotting.

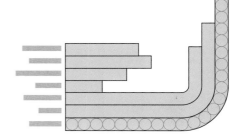

Right This graphic solution effectively employs three charts, one to show the low values and the others for the high values. The apparent folding that connects the charts accentuates the value differences.

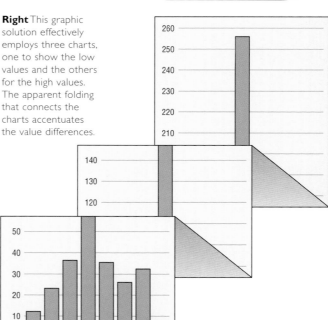

Left An acutely angled projection may be all you need to fit a bar if it is not so much greater than the others.

Right There are
various methods of
displaying negative
values clearly in a bar
chart. The most
common one, shown
in this example, has
the baseline set part
way up the chart,
so that the negatives
can be displayed as
inverse bars.

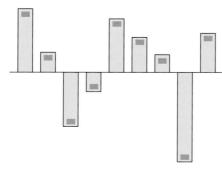

Right If all the values
in the data set are
high, you may want to
have the chart base
at a higher value than
zero, so that the
bar differentiation is
enhanced. To make
it clear that the chart
has a non-zero base,
you can draw the
bars starting off the
chart edge.

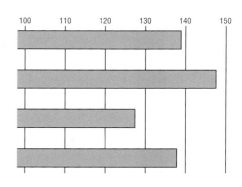

Right In order to
maximize the heights
of positive bars, you
can just leave gaps in
the chart where the
negative values occur.

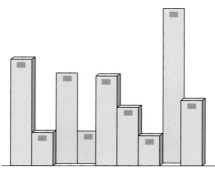

Right A graphic
device like this fold
effect in the chart
also draws attention
to a non-zero base.

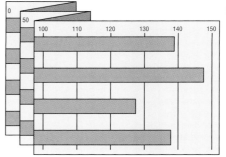

Right This method
shows the height
of the negative values
as flat bars. The
advantage is that the
negative values are
visualized effectively
but are still clearly
different from the
other bars.

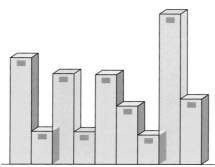

Right This alternative
to the one above also
shows the heights of
the negative values
in position within the
chart, but here they
are drawn to appear
as transparent bars.

Right Here we have
a folded chart drawn
in perspective. This
really exaggerates the
distortion, while still
presenting the data
effectively.

69

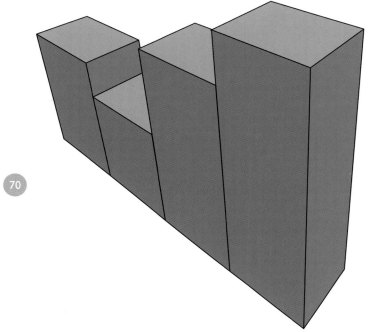

Left Dramatic 3-D effects will give impact to your bar charts. This chart was initially plotted as a basic outline using vector drawing software. Paths were then exported to be manipulated and rendered in a 3-D program.

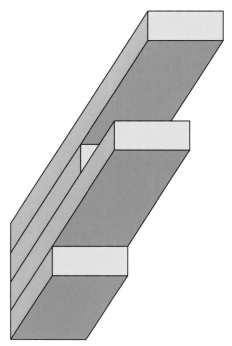

Right Based on the same data, the outline of this version was drawn in its final shape using vector software. The lines were then imported into a retouching program to be colored. As it is based on an oblique projection, it has the advantage of being measurable.

Right Here are several ways in which you can pick out or highlight particular bars in a chart if the general pattern, based on the data, makes all the bars very similar.

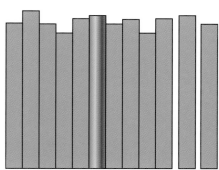

Right You may want to add character to your charts by using pictorial elements that have a more informal, cartoon-like treatment.

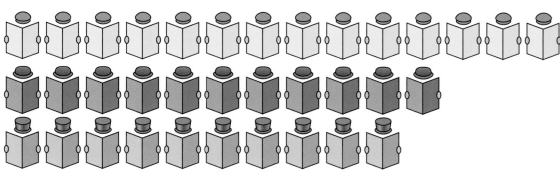

Right A chart like this definitely carries visual impact, and is not so difficult to achieve with currently available software, clip art, and a little imagination. It could be used to represent a whole range of travel-related activities.

Right Here a familiar object is used as the bar. The cassette is created out of a few circles and lines, and the film strip is even simpler.

Right This example demonstrates how a photographic image placed behind a simple bar chart can create a great effect. Thousands of suitable royalty-free images are now available as clip art.

Right A photograph serves as the base for this chart too. The image was imported into a vector drawing program, and bars made up of the flame icon were superimposed in order to create an arresting image.

Major outbreaks

1980
1985
1990
1995
2000

STATISTICAL DIAGRAMS / AREA CHARTS I

Area charts are most recognizable in the form of the pie chart, so called because it resembles a pie cut into radial slices. Yet there are other forms of area chart, some of them definitely easier to create and label than the familiar pie. Whereas bar charts show values as one-dimensional length, area charts show values as areas. This requires a little calculation. The area of a rectangle is length times width. That of a triangle is half the height times the base. The area of a circle is pi times the radius squared (πr^2). With pie charts we need concern ourselves only with the divisions—converting the total value to 360° and making the angles of the segments divisions of that. Fortunately, spreadsheet and drawing software programs usually have a pie chart-creating facility. Also, the mathematical equations needed to calculate areas are easy and, with the aid of a computer should present no problem at all.

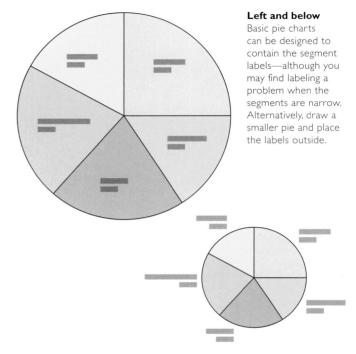

Left and below
Basic pie charts can be designed to contain the segment labels—although you may find labeling a problem when the segments are narrow. Alternatively, draw a smaller pie and place the labels outside.

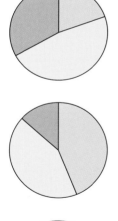

Left With two or more pie charts to show as a group, you need to decide how to arrange them. If you keep them separate, you should be able to fit labels easily. Try to use the same start point, such as the top vertical, for the first segment in a repeating series.

Below If you overlap pie charts (which has the merit of saving space), make sure you don't obscure too much of the overlaid pies. You can use a key to identify the segments, but leave enough space on the charts to show the value labels.

Right Pie charts are often compressed vertically to create an elliptical outline, which takes up less space. However, this does distort the area and so is potentially misleading, particularly for narrow segments, as is clear from these examples.

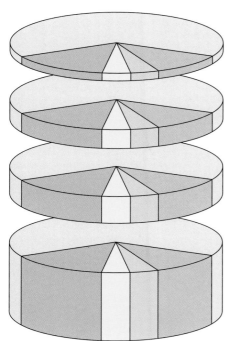

Left Adding a front edge to an elliptical or circular pie chart creates a 3-D effect, but don't make it too deep. The pie is an area chart—and as the edge is added only to the front, segments that are given an edge will have a greater visual area, especially when the same color is used. Making the edge colors markedly darker or using a different color will lessen the distortion.

Left Although circular area charts usually take the form of a divided pie, you can use circles with a variety of areas to create another form of area chart. The area of a circle is πr^2. Divide a value, say 42, by π (3.142) = 13.37. This is r^2, so find the square root of 13.37 (which is 3.65) and that's the radius of a circle of area 42. Work out the radii for all the other items in your data set and draw all the circles. You can enlarge or reduce the circles as a group, maintaining their proportions. You can also resize them in one dimension to create ellipses.

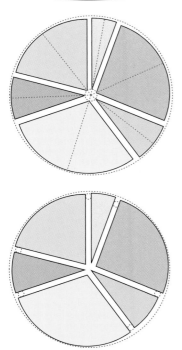

Left Separating the segments to create an "exploded" pie is a popular technique. As the pie segments will usually vary in size, moving them an equal amount radially out from the center will produce uneven gaps between segments. However, keeping an even separation means that segments have to be moved varying distances from the center. The choice is yours.

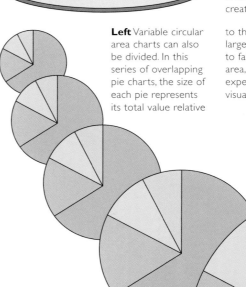

Left Variable circular area charts can also be divided. In this series of overlapping pie charts, the size of each pie represents its total value relative to the others. The largest pie is allowed to fall off the page area, the reader being expected to mentally visualize the full chart.

STATISTICAL DIAGRAMS / AREA CHARTS 2

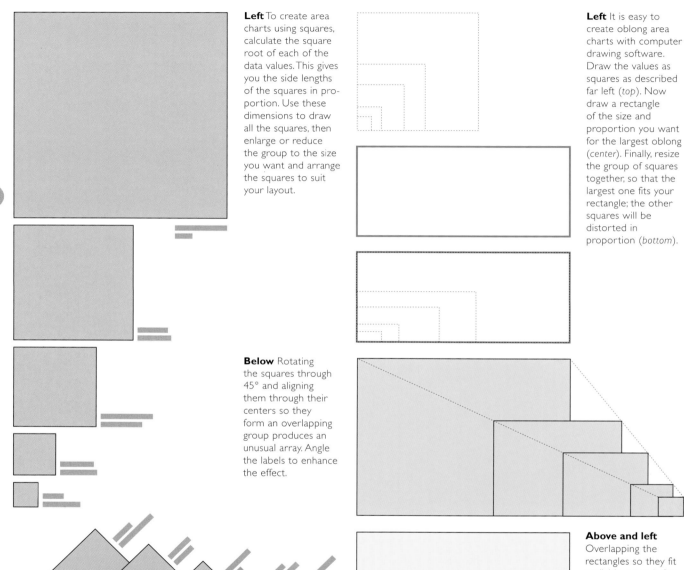

Left To create area charts using squares, calculate the square root of each of the data values. This gives you the side lengths of the squares in proportion. Use these dimensions to draw all the squares, then enlarge or reduce the group to the size you want and arrange the squares to suit your layout.

Left It is easy to create oblong area charts with computer drawing software. Draw the values as squares as described far left (*top*). Now draw a rectangle of the size and proportion you want for the largest oblong (*center*). Finally, resize the group of squares together, so that the largest one fits your rectangle; the other squares will be distorted in proportion (*bottom*).

Below Rotating the squares through 45° and aligning them through their centers so they form an overlapping group produces an unusual array. Angle the labels to enhance the effect.

Above and left Overlapping the rectangles so they fit available space is fine, as long as you leave adequate space for labels. Using a hard or soft shadow helps to separate the shapes visually.

Right Having created your rectangles to the correct proportion, you can use digital techniques to adjust the shapes—by shearing, for example. Experiment with unusual arrangements to make the charts stimulating.

Right This effective (but false) perspective was created in a vector program. After being rotated, each rectangle was resized on the vertical axis only and by varying amounts. The visible areas are distorted, but for conveying a general idea this is acceptable.

Below Even regular flat squares can be set out interestingly. The arrangement shown here works well when the chart has to be integrated with a text layout.

Right Even triangles can be used as area charts. Simply create square areas, using the square roots of the data values. Now delete one corner point of each square to make the triangles and resize them as a group, in proportion, to produce the shape you want.

Below Instead of using a single shape to represent a value, you can use multiple units. This type of diagram, a unit area chart, gives you flexibility in arranging the pattern for each entry.

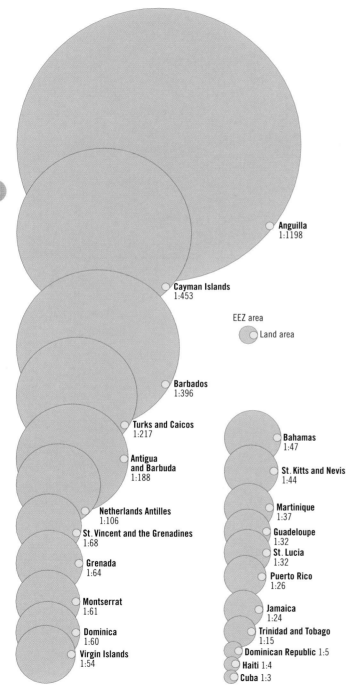

Anguilla
1:1198

Cayman Islands
1:453

EEZ area
Land area

Barbados
1:396

Turks and Caicos
1:217

Antigua
and Barbuda
1:188

Netherlands Antilles
1:106

St. Vincent and the Grenadines
1:68

Grenada
1:64

Montserrat
1:61

Dominica
1:60

Virgin Islands
1:54

Bahamas
1:47

St. Kitts and Nevis
1:44

Martinique
1:37

Guadeloupe
1:32

St. Lucia
1:32

Puerto Rico
1:26

Jamaica
1:24

Trinidad and Tobago
1:15

Dominican Republic 1:5

Haiti 1:4

Cuba 1:3

Left In this chart the various areas have been shown against a common benchmark value that remains a constant size. The subject matter is sea area as a proportion of the land areas of islands, but there are other applications.

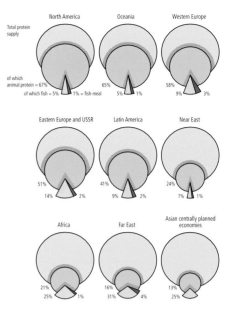

Total protein supply

of which animal protein = 67%

of which fish = 5%   1% = fish-meal

North America   Oceania   Western Europe

65%   5%   1%   58%   9%   3%

Eastern Europe and USSR   Latin America   Near East

51%   14%   2%   41%   9%   2%   24%   7%   1%

Africa   Far East   Asian centrally planned economies

21%   25%   1%   16%   31%   4%   13%   25%

Right This diagram combines circular area charts with divided area (pie) charts. The rearmost circle represents the 100% total for each region.

Right Juxtaposing two half pies that vary in size according to their totals is a neat way of stressing the comparison and saving space, too.

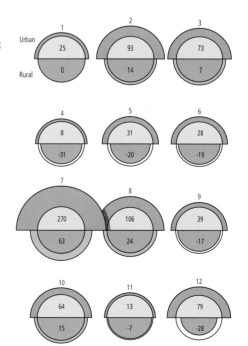

	1	2	3
Urban	25	93	73
Rural	0	14	7

	4	5	6
	8	31	28
	-31	-20	-19

	7	8	9
	270	106	39
	63	24	-17

	10	11	12
	64	13	79
	15	-7	-28

Right Rectangular area charts can include subdivisions. These split area charts are easier to construct than pie charts, and can be just as effective. Don't overlap charts like these, as the labels could easily be misread.

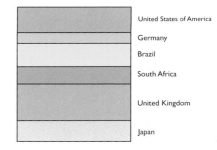

Above In each of the charts in this series, percentages are shown as sections of the full area. You can add interest to a chart drawn from a bland set of data by using an unusual projection and then offsetting a segment, in this case vertically.

Right Royalty-free photographic images can be dropped into rectangular, circular, or other shapes used for area charts. But make sure they are still clearly charts and aren't mistaken for odd-shaped pictures.

Right Angle split area charts to create a more interesting layout. Construct the charts initially as basic rectangles, then use a shearing process in the vector drawing program to achieve the angle you want.

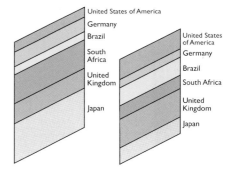

Right This variation of the split area chart works when there are three conditions to be shown, one of which can be treated separately. In this case the "not sure" value is isolated so that the "yes/no" comparison is more easily seen.

STATISTICAL DIAGRAMS / VOLUME CHARTS I

V olume charts are slightly more complicated than area
charts to calculate, but they are particularly useful
when comparing data vastly different in value.

A bar might be drawn to a width of 10cm; an
area 10cm square contains 100cm²; but a cube measuring
10cm × 10cm × 10cm holds 1000cm³. So long as the
shape will be recognized as a cube, it can represent ten
times the value conveyed by the area chart without
taking up much more page space.

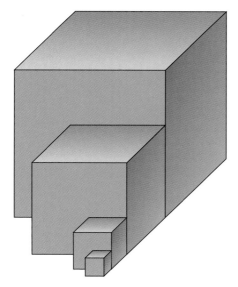

Left These examples
demonstrate how
volume charts are
able to represent
vastly greater values
in a compact space.
Bar charts use only
one dimension to
express value, and
these bars equate to
(from the top down)
40, 25, 10, and 5 units.
Square area charts
represent values as
a multiple of width ×
height, and in this
case show 1600, 625,
100, and 25 units.
Because the volume
chart uses three
dimensions (width ×
height × depth), these
four cubes represent
values of 64,000,
15,625, 1000, and 125
respectively.

Right Choose the
projection for volume
that suits your design
requirements best.
These examples are
based on angles of
30°, 45°, and 60°.
You can also use any
oblique projection.

Above These three
shapes—the cube,
the sphere, and the
cylinder—all have
calculable volumes,
which makes them
suitable for volume
charts. The cube and
the cylinder can be
drawn convincingly
in line, but all three
benefit from some
careful shading.

The volume of
a cube is:
width × height ×
depth.
That of a sphere is:
$(4 \times \pi \times r^3) \div 3$.
And the volume of
a cylinder is:
$\pi \times r^2 \times height$
(or length).

For most general
calculation, $\pi = 3.142$.

The cylinder and the
cube are the easiest
volumes to calculate
and draw, but the
sphere is also used.
Its most common
application is in
showing the compar-
ative sizes of planets
and stars.

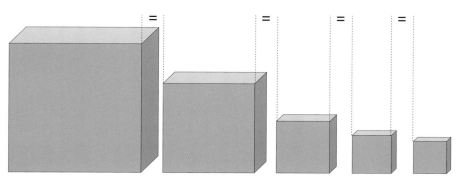

Left You will need to give some thought to the best arrangement for a series of volume blocks. Keep in mind where labels will fit. You can abut the blocks or space them evenly, aligning them at either the front edge or back edge.

Below Volume charts can create striking images—particularly when given imaginative color treatment, as in this example. The underlit effect adds drama to a powerful structure.

Left Volume charts can be set out in a wide variety of ways, so experiment with various methods. If you choose to "stack" the blocks, you could keep the chart compact by aligning the top and back edges so that they fit within the top face of the base block. Otherwise you can place them so the base (obscured) corners align. But remember to leave sufficient space for labels.

STATISTICAL DIAGRAMS / VOLUME CHARTS 2

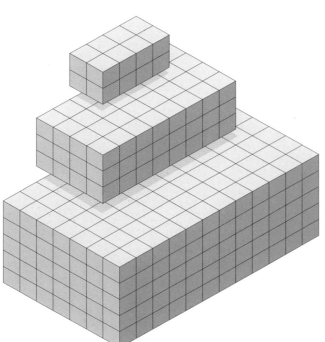

Left Volume charts can be made up from even-sized cubic units. This unit-volume chart has the advantage of a grid that enables the user to measure values. The charts are simple to construct in a vector drawing program. Just draw one small cube, then duplicate it to build the larger cubes. You'll find that using a regular angle, such as 30° or 45°, is helpful.

Right A grid base makes a very effective background for these cube structures.

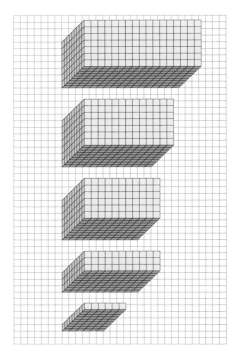

Left You don't have to stick to an overall cube shape for the unit-volume chart. In fact, provided you are working with small numbers of cubes, the style is very flexible and allows you to build shapes to suit your needs.

Right Here, unit-volume blocks drawn to an isometric format are laid out in a random pattern conforming to an isometric grid base, adding interest to the design.

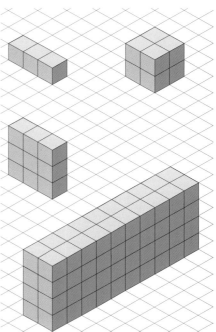

Right Since the blocks have a built-in measurable grid structure, you don't have to use complete blocks. You can take out one or more of the individual units. This not only makes an interesting shape, but can be a very useful way of drawing attention to the differences between data values. The upper example is based on a complete cube with blocks removed. In the lower chart, the basis is a linear group. The removal of blocks in the subsequent groups is done in a systematic way, so as to facilitate understanding.

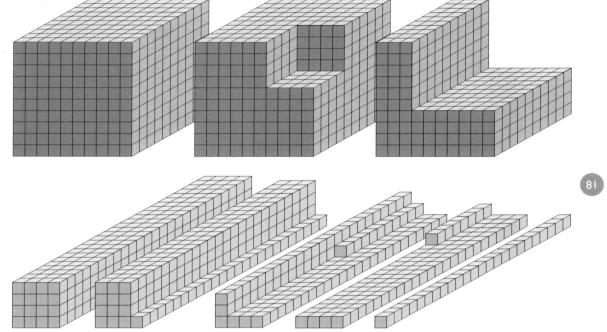

Right Using 3-D software, you can produce eye-catching arrangements of unit-volume charts. Just make sure that the reader can see enough of the blocks to make an adequate visual comparison.

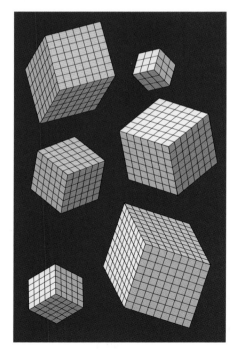

Right Other shapes that you can use to make unit-volume charts include the cylinder and the sphere, which are then built up to form essentially cubic shapes—since making a cylinder or sphere of the units would be asking too much of the reader.

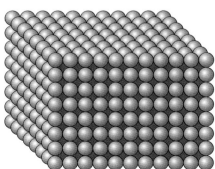

STATISTICAL DIAGRAMS / VOLUME CHARTS 3

Left Volume charts plotted using a two-point perspective projection—in which the vertical sides remain parallel—have an impressive solidity. Use a 3-D drawing program to create them, as they would be difficult to create accurately using standard 2-D vector drawing software. The sides of the cubes can be used to display an identifying graphic element— such as a pictogram of the subject, or a map.

Left Three-point perspective produces even more convincing shapes, but you have to be careful not to make the view too extreme. Otherwise, users will not be able to make a sensible comparison of data— which is the point of the chart. The degree of distortion is indicated by the red dotted outline. This shows how the lowest cube would appear if plotted on the plane of the top cube. Charts like these need to be created in a 3-D program to obtain correct proportions.

Right Three-point perspective can be used for unit-volume charts, too. This example shows how information is distorted. Because the removed segment is drawn forward in the same plane, it appears much larger than the space it has vacated. However, the unit grid allows a fair comparison to be made.

Right A volume chart that has the blocks in perspective and randomly oriented creates interest—but if the blocks overlap, you can create the wrong impression of size. These three examples are all made from the same set of cubes. Notice how the overlaps make the cubes appear to vary in size. In the bottom example the grid provides the reader with a visual control mechanism, making comparison and assimilation of values easier.

Below In this chart showing sizes of stars, the largest value is much greater than all the others. Had the chart been designed to show the largest volume in its entirety, the others would have been minute and indistinguishable in size. Because most of the largest volume has been allowed to fall off the edge of the page, the others appear at a useful size. The curve of the edge of the biggest volume is sufficient to suggest its massive scale to the reader.

83

STATISTICAL DIAGRAMS / COMBINED CHARTS I

In order to introduce some dynamism into a relatively dull array of charts, you can combine two or more different chart types. Almost any statistical diagrams can be successfully combined, with a little imagination and ingenuity. Make sure that any color-coded identity is maintained across the chart styles and that scale grids cannot be confused.

Adjusted total (US$millions)

Variable rate
Flat rate

Fiscal year

Right Combining one or more line graphs with a bar chart is quite straightforward, especially if the scale grid applies to all the elements in the chart. Make sure you clearly label each line or bar —a key is particularly useful for this.

Left When the charts need different scale grids, you have to make certain that the reader will easily locate the relevant grid for each element. Associated colored lines and type aid the visual link.

Right In this design, unit-area charts are combined with the labels of a simple split bar chart. The leader lines serve both to link the labels to the bar charts—very useful for the shallow bar segments—and to provide a matrix for the unit-area charts.

Millions of US dollars

Host-government contributions 1 164.9

World Bank/IDA 628.3 21 projects
Asia Development Bank 254.8 4 projects
African Development Bank 89.2 6 projects
IFAD 23.5 5 projects
UN High Commission for Refugees 20.0 1 project
Inter-American Development Bank 8.0 1 project
Corporación Andina de Fomento 3.9 1 project
FAO/Bankers Programme 2.4 1 project
UNDP/Netherlands 1.4 1 project
Other co-financing 112.7

Total investments 2 309.1   Total 41 projects

Residual value / Outstanding rentals / Market value

Right You can use secondary charts to show subsets of data. Here the vertical 3-D bar chart is the dominant element, and the 2-D horizontal charts—which supply the breakdown of information—are color-coordinated for easy reference.

Below The angled arrangement of these bar and area charts helps hold each group together as a unit. This allows you to use the colors to distinguish the type of chart content, rather than for identifying each country.

85

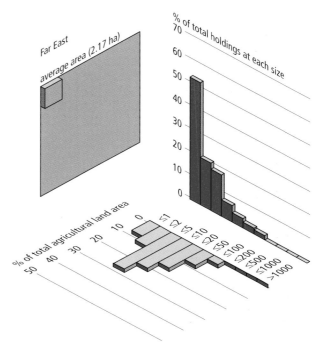

STATISTICAL DIAGRAMS / COMBINED CHARTS 2

Right You can show the makeup of one segment of a pie area chart like this, by extending the depth of the segment. In fact, two split-column charts are combined with each segment to show the breakdown of the segment value by two methods.

Far right This chart combines a pie and bar diagram also, but each segment is given a column value. Note that the data forming the height values is different from the segment proportions. Arrange the chart so that the tallest columns appear at the back.

1990
15%
28,220
37,470
23,280
63,500
96,000   145,470

1995
18%
24,690
47,270
72,670
84,870
113,595   148,370

2000
12%
67,560
83,250
76,200
102,300
142,520   132,110

N. America — Export
Europe — Wheat
Africa — Coarse grains
— Milled rice   *figures in tonnes*

31%
640
24%
452
17%
337
8%
284
12%
245
8%
143

Right A third method of combining pie and bar charts allows the pie to appear as a full circle on the face of the bar. The bars vary in length, according to total value, and segments of the bar show an alternative breakdown of the total values.

86

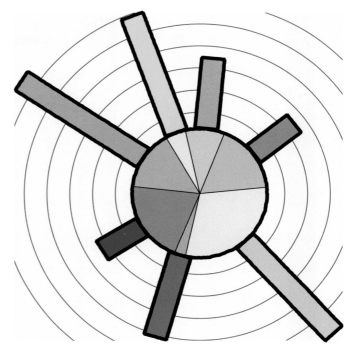

Left You can also add bars to a regular pie by simply using the circumference as a base. By keeping the bars narrow and adding a top marker, you can fit bars to even the narrowest segment—but you'll have to rotate the chart to get the best fit in the design area.

Right Here, bigger segments allow bars to be drawn at a broader measure. Using the circular grid device, you can dispense with actual values for the bar totals.

Left and right These further variations of the simple pie/bar arrangement place a grid around the bars. By offsetting the grid units, you can make them look like stacks of coins—obviously used only when the bars represent monetary values.

STATISTICAL DIAGRAMS / COMBINED CHARTS 3

Right In this volume chart and divided bar chart combination, the rightmost bar serves as a key to the divisions for all the bars. This allows you to keep the blocks close together and thus get visual value for the volume dimension.

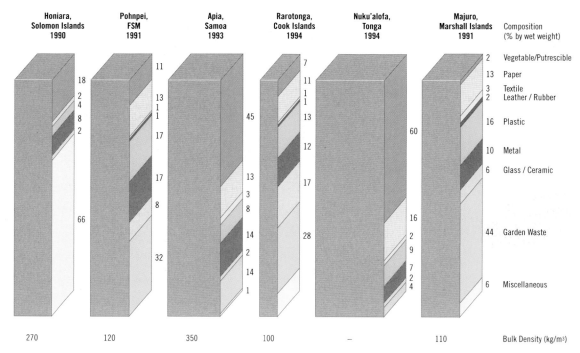

	Honiara, Solomon Islands 1990	Pohnpei, FSM 1991	Apia, Samoa 1993	Rarotonga, Cook Islands 1994	Nuku'alofa, Tonga 1994	Majuro, Marshall Islands 1991	Composition (% by wet weight)
		11		7		2	Vegetable/Putrescible
	18	13		11		13	Paper
	2	1		1		3	Textile
	4	1		1		2	Leather / Rubber
	8	17	45	13		16	Plastic
	2				60		
		17		12		10	Metal
			13			6	Glass / Ceramic
		17	3	17			
		8	8				
	66				16	44	Garden Waste
		14	28		2		
		2			9		
		32	14		7		
			1		2		
					4	6	Miscellaneous

Bulk Density (kg/m³)	270	120	350	100	–	110	

Right This decorative arrangement of unit-area and variable-area pie charts allows a detailed level of information to be shown. The units are color-coordinated, with the pie segments enabling the reader to make the association immediately.

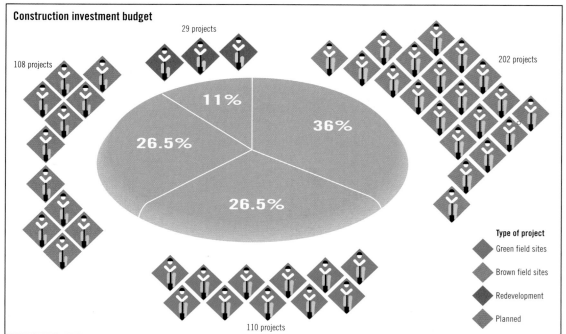

Construction investment budget

29 projects

108 projects

202 projects

11%

36%

26.5%

26.5%

110 projects

Type of project
- Green field sites
- Brown field sites
- Redevelopment
- Planned

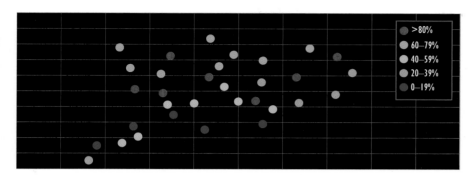

Left Color use is invaluable as an aid to identification. You can also use it to show values. In this scatter chart, a color scale lists the values that the color circles represent. This adds to the information given on the chart's x and y axes.

Below If color is a problem, scatter graphs can show the third value as an area chart. The circles are centered on the plot point of the x/y coordinates, and the size of the circles varies according to the third value.

89

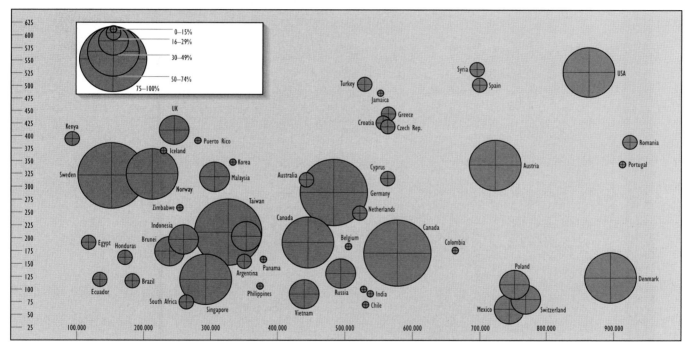

Right Color is used in this chart, too, to show value. The height of each bar represents average rainfall each week over a year in a particular area, while the color of the bar shows the average temperature for the same period.

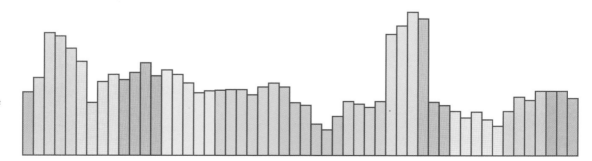

RELATIONAL DIAGRAMS I

Relational diagrams illustrate the physical association or juxtaposition of objects, animate or inanimate, in the physical world. Most commonly these diagrams are maps, plans, or charts, in the traditional sense; but they also include signage that tells you, usually in a tabular format, how you relate to particular surroundings—in other words, your position.

Plans are probably the oldest kind of graphic device, being an essential tool both for local and more universal navigation. Current navigational techniques make use of artificial-satellite systems and other scientific facilities, yet still depend on visual displays for their functionality. We need to "picture" where we are.

This section attempts to cover a vast and extremely diverse range of information-design potential in a few pages. It cannot be comprehensive, but should serve as a concise practical guide for the information designer.

Right In its simplest form, the relational diagram indicates the direction in which an object lies in relation to the potential user. This caption starts with the word "right"—which informs you, the reader, that the object described lies in that direction from this starting point.

Left In its simplest form, the relational diagram indicates the direction in which an object lies in relation to the potential user. This caption starts with the word "left"—which informs you, the reader, that the object described lies in that direction from this starting point.

Right Clear symbols are more visible from a distance than text is, and can be used to clarify text. If they are used as a substitute for written information, their meaning must be unmistakable – particularly where users may travel some distance before realizing their error.

Right Direction signs are basic relational diagrams. As with all information design, they need careful consideration if they are to function efficiently. Take into account where they will be positioned, and the distance from which they are likely to be viewed. A good sign is clearly visible; the content is legible and unambiguous. Direction signs will usually include one or more arrows.

Right Highway route indicators are a good example of graphic design based on an accepted language. The starting point (the user's position) is always at the base; the current route is drawn on a vertical axis, points upward, and ends with an arrowhead at the top; subsidiary routes extend from this main route and include labels to identify key locations. This basic design can be used in other contexts to show route options. Keep in mind that the majority of users may have little or no knowledge of local geography.

City and Northeast District Hospital

3RD FLOOR

◄ REDWOOD WARD

◄ OAK WARD

◄ MAPLE WARD

◄ BIRCHWOOD WARD

DAY CARE ►

EYE CLINIC ►

RADIOLOGY ►

J30 M18
Chesterfield
Dronfield
Sheffield J29
Mansfield
Ollerton
J28
Eastwood
Heanor J27
Nottingham
Hucknall
J26
Beeston
West Bridgford
J25
Donnington
Derby J24

Right Inside public transport vehicles, visible display space is usually horizontal. Line diagrams have to fit to this, and usually simplify the route to a straight line between the terminal points. Legibility is vital, given the often crowded and unsteady state of a mobile vehicle.

Right In transport route diagrams, the routes shown will often need to include branch options. With careful design, detailed information can be included— but limit the variety of items shown, and include a clear key.

Right The simplest maps tend to be limited to locational relationships. The maps here not only show the locational relationship but also indicate travel distance, travel time, and travel cost as comparative lengths of line.

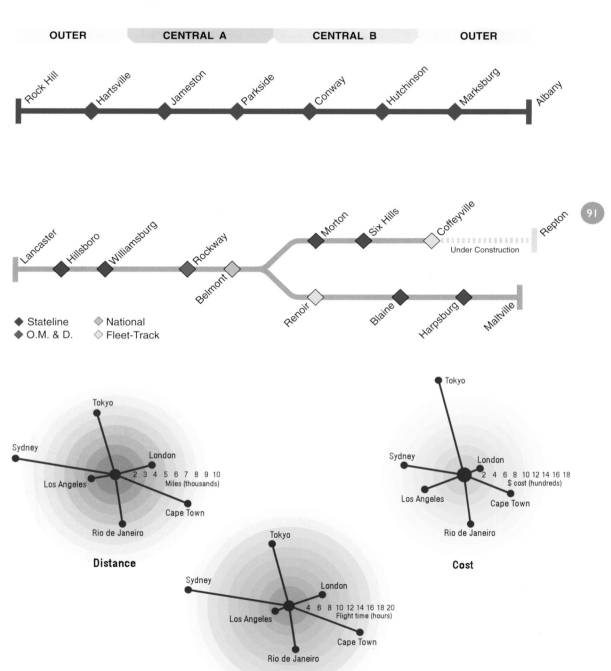

RELATIONAL DIAGRAMS 2

Right Plans are the most localized form of mapping. In a basic 2-D floor plan, areas are delineated, the line thickness varying to distinguish wall types. Other features are shown in simple geometric form.

Right Adding height to the wall introduces the third dimension and transforms the plan, giving the reader a stronger visual idea of the structure. Additional items, such as stairs, become a little trickier to draw, but the overall result is more solid.

Right You can further enhance the 3-D effect by adding tones of color to the walls and floor areas.

Right Working to a nonperspective projection makes it easier to do the drawing with 2-D software. You could use any angle, but established projections such as the isometric or oblique projections (see page 60) are most effective.

Below Resizing the vertical scale of a 3-D floor plan to varying degrees gives a good perspective effect. You'll need to adjust the wall depths.

Right Take care when adding labels to plan drawings. Don't obscure locations or overwrite the line structure. Keep labels off the plan area so that the leader lines do not visually interrupt the type.

Left This projected drawing gives the user an overview of the building. The color coding enables the user to locate general areas, then examine the detail on the enlarged floor plan. The function of the keyed numbering system is to identify specific locations.

RELATIONAL DIAGRAMS 3

Right Local relational diagrams in the form of street maps need careful preparation. Streets must be drawn so that they relate to each other, but can be simplified to a considerable extent. The examples here range from the realistic to a stylized geometric treatment.

Right How you draw the actual street lines is a matter of style. A tint base suggests a built-up area with white streets. Draw a wide black line and superimpose a cloned but thinner white line to obtain parallel road edges.

Right Labels usually follow the line of the street. Drawing software allows you to attach type to invisible paths formed by cloned street lines. Don't rotate type through more than 90°.

Right All too often you'll find that street names are longer than the streets on the plan. Leader lines and abbreviations will help. You'll also find that several names appear along one stretch of street. If the names are close together, try using a separating device.

Right A matrix of grid lines dividing a large plan into smaller units, combined with a street index, helps the reader locate streets on complex maps. Make sure the grid lines are clear, but don't interrupt or confuse the lines of the streets.

Right It is generally accepted that maps and plans are drawn with north at the top. If your map is rotated, you should indicate this by using a grid or a north pointer. Most maps will need some form of scale of distance (remember to include the scale in any change of size).

Cultural Heritage and Infrastructure Projects in the Historic Core of Bethlehem

Salesian Church

Lutheran Church

Paul VI St

Greek Orthodox Church

Salesian St.

Star St

at-Tarajme St.

Star St.

Syrian Orthodox Church

Farahiye St.

Fawagire St.

al-Qana' St.

Najaire St.

Market

Paul VI St.

Manger Square

al-Anatre St.

Milk Grotto St.

Armenian Church

Catholic Church St. Catherine

Church of Nativity

Greek Orthodox Church

Coptic and Ethiopian Church

Rehabilitation projects funded by different donors

- Sweden
- Germany
- Belgium
- Spain
- Japan
- Greece
- France

Left Once you have drawn the basic street plan you can incorporate other information. Color will obviously aid visual differentiation of areas or streets.

95

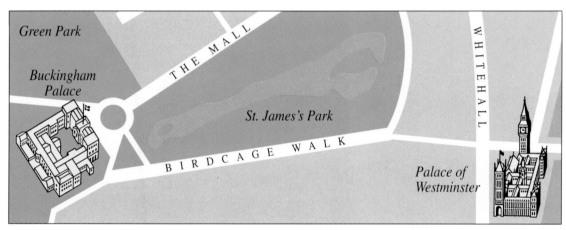

Green Park

Buckingham Palace

THE MALL

St. James's Park

BIRDCAGE WALK

WHITEHALL

Palace of Westminster

Left Pictograms are a good way of adding interest to a simple street plan.

1 Buckingham Palace and Canada gate.
7 cameras (9 positions)

2 Clarence House and the Mall.
5 Cameras

3 Trafalgar Square.
3 Cameras

Clarence House

St James Palace

Duke of York steps

KG VI

The Mall

Trafalgar Square

Northumberland Avenue

1

2

3

Left Keep the representation of streets as simple as possible on diagrams such as this, which serve only as a background to locate particular activities. Buildings, too, are shown in simple geometric form.

RELATIONAL DIAGRAMS 4

Right Sometimes you will need to show information at local area level together with a wider overview. Rather than attempting to show the detail on a single map, you could use two or more maps with different scales. At each level, the next stage map is shown as an inset area. Varying the size of the map, with the biggest map being the main focus, creates an interesting arrangement. For a more dynamic effect, you can rotate and angle the maps.

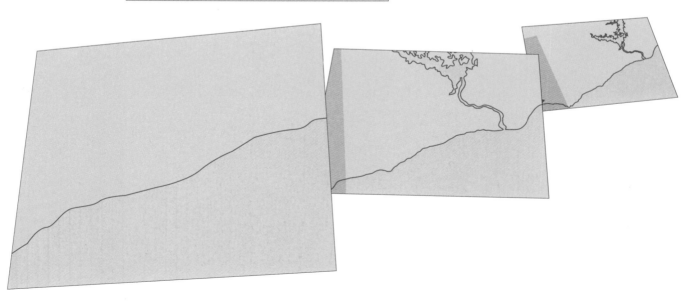

Right Stylize map detail by plotting it along a geometric grid. In this example, all lines change direction in multiples of 45°. This departs from the actual geographical form, but creates a striking graphic effect.

Below Use of strong color produces eye-catching maps. Here, the map detail has been limited to items of relevance to the subject. The inset map locates the large-scale map in a broader geographical context.

Right In this map, too, the content is restricted to relevant subject matter. The underlying tonal base, indicating topographic structure, enhances the simple treatment of the other items.

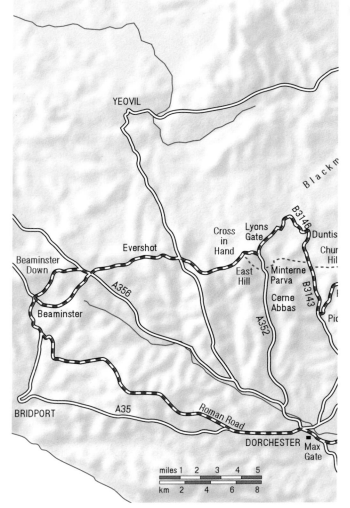

RELATIONAL DIAGRAMS 5

Right and below

Maps at the global level present particular problems for the information designer. The world is (almost) spherical. At lower levels, areas can be assumed to be flat and evenly scaled in either dimension. Mapping at this level requires a basic understanding of geography in order to avoid pitfalls.

Right and below

To draw usable maps of the 3-D globe in two dimensions, cartographers have devised all sorts of projections. Each one is a compromise, distorting land areas to a greater or lesser extent. Designers must select the most appropriate one for their needs.

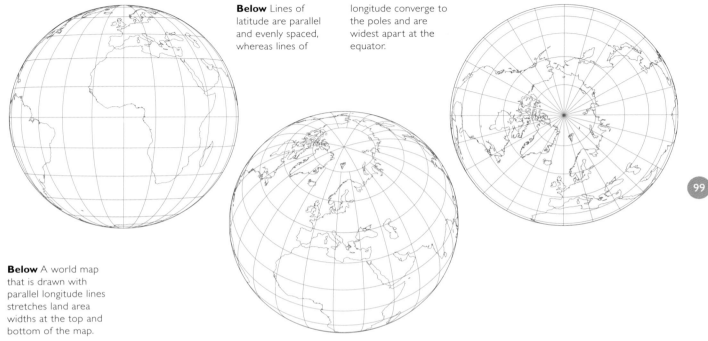

Below Lines of latitude are parallel and evenly spaced, whereas lines of longitude converge to the poles and are widest apart at the equator.

Below A world map that is drawn with parallel longitude lines stretches land area widths at the top and bottom of the map.

RELATIONAL DIAGRAMS 6

Right Because reality has to be edited to work on the 2-D page, all mapping is a compromise. You will need to decide the level of editing to suit the use. If too much detail is drawn, it will fill in and look ugly, so keep in mind the size at which it will be reproduced.

Right These examples shows some of the many styles you can use for coastlines. Unlike the cartographer, the information designer can experiment to obtain striking results. Digital technology facilitates such testing.

Right Lakes, rivers, and other waterways can be treated in a variety of ways, although readers tend to associate blue with water.

Right You can show hills and mountains by symbols. Trees, too, can be represented by icons. Larger areas of woodland can be shown by color.

Right Regional and national boundaries can be drawn as lines. You might need to use a different style to show disputed national borders, of which there are many. Alternatively, just distinguish areas by color fill.

Right Various line styles (both treatment and color) are used to represent roads and other transport links. Be consistent in line thickness for types of road. Draw parallel lines digitally by superimposing a duplicated line over the original and making it narrower.

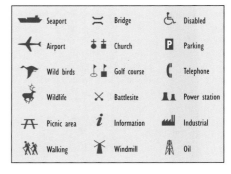

Right Town locations may be represented by dots on small-scale maps, or by patches of tint simulating the urban shape on large-scale ones. You can vary the size or style of dot to indicate the size or significance of the town.

Settlement/hamlet
Small town/village
Large town
Small city
Major city
CAPITAL
Town name
Urban area
Town name
Town name
Town name
Town name
Urban area
Town name
Town name
City center
Town name
Town name
Town name

Right You can use icons to locate other significant points. There are fonts that include wide collections of appropriate symbols, or you can devise your own. Just make sure that they will read at the size at which they are to be reproduced.

Seaport	Bridge	Disabled
Airport	Church	Parking
Wild birds	Golf course	Telephone
Wildlife	Battlesite	Power station
Picnic area	Information	Industrial
Walking	Windmill	Oil

Right A compass point is useful, particularly if the map is not north-oriented. Most maps benefit from the inclusion of a scale. This needs to be long enough for the reader to make sensible use of it, but not so long as to intrude on the map detail.

Miles 1 2 3 4 5
Kilometres 1 2 3 4 5 6 7 8
Miles 1 2 3 4 5
Kilometres 1 2 3 4 5 6 7 8
Miles 1 2 3 4 5
Kilometres 1 2 3 4 5 6 7 8

Right You may want to finish your map with a simple single line frame, or you could give it a little extra style with a more elaborate edge. The frame can also be used as a clipping path, to tidy up roads and other lines that overlap the edge.

RELATIONAL DIAGRAMS 7

Right The same map, different effects—all achieved by means of digital manipulation.

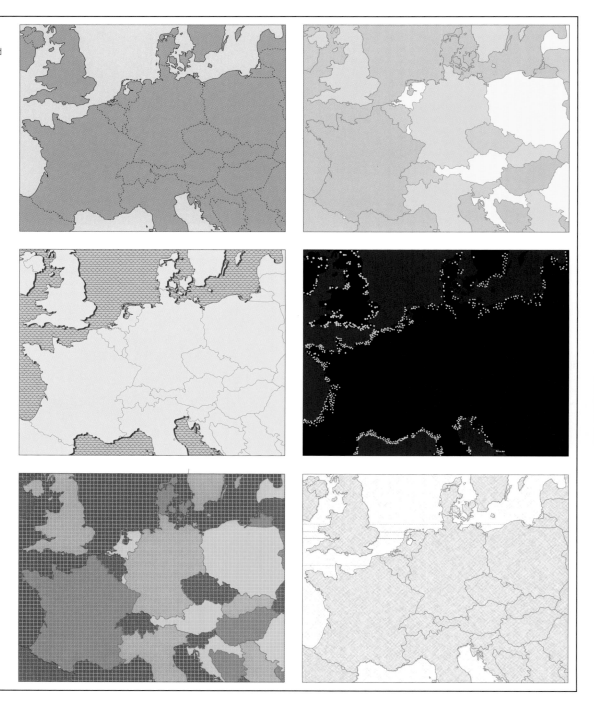

Right You can create striking images with perspective effects generated by digital manipulation.

Right Less dramatic, but equally effective, is this "antique" styling. The lines are made uneven and a hand-drawn font is used for type labels in order to achieve the effect.

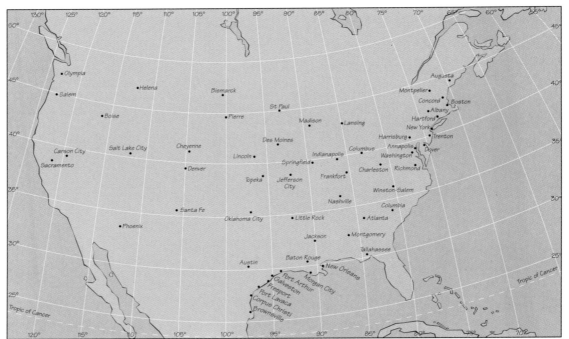

RELATIONAL DIAGRAMS 8

Contours show height variations. This cross-section through a mountain has a vertical scale of heights. If lines are drawn on the surface, where the scale touches you can see the linear pattern of contours.

Right Using the contour lines, you can show different heights by color. A common convention in atlases, this can be used to great effect by the information designer.

Right Another fairly standard convention in atlases is the addition of shading. This usually assumes a light source at top left. It needs to be subtle if labels and other graphic matter are to be legible.

Right This unusual but effective treatment is obtained by adding a soft shadow to the underside of each contour level.

Right Hachures were used extensively to show topographic information in atlases of hand-drawn maps. Although effective, they are very time-consuming to create, even digitally.

Right You can render realistic terrain by using "digital elevation models" (DEMs). Data for these is freely available from various sources on the Web. The converted data provides a grayscale image—white is high, black low.

Right Using the "Lighting Effects" feature of an image-editing application such as Adobe Photoshop, you can use a grayscale DEM as a "bump map" to render a realistic terrain view.

Right Check out the graphic capabilities of your spreadsheet program. Some are able to display and manipulate contour information derived from *X-Y-Z* coordinates, such as in this image of Mount Everest. Once compiled, the image can then be angled and rotated as you wish.

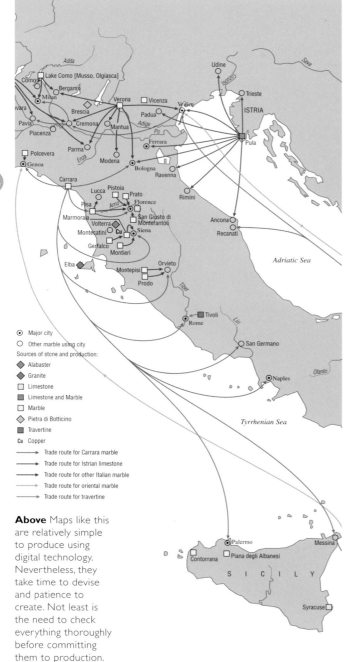

Above Maps like this are relatively simple to produce using digital technology. Nevertheless, they take time to devise and patience to create. Not least is the need to check everything thoroughly before committing them to production.

Below Maps serve as an informative base for other information graphics. These circular bar diagrams benefit from a visual geographical context.

Above
Here again the
map contributes
to the available
information,
located by leader
lines and color
coding.

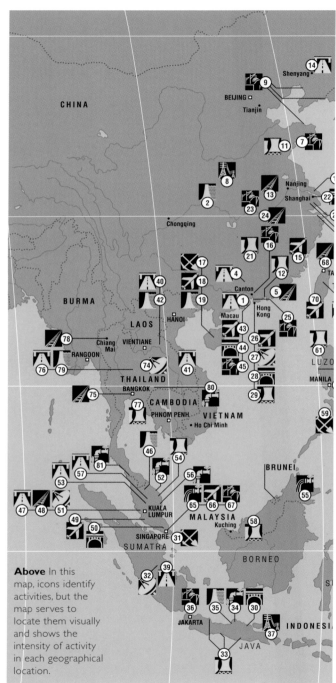

Above In this
map, icons identify
activities, but the
map serves to
locate them visually
and shows the
intensity of activity
in each geographical
location.

ORGANIZATIONAL DIAGRAMS I

Whereas relational charts are used to illustrate a general pattern of links, organizational diagrams show specific interrelationships between items. These items need not be physical entities; they can be abstract concepts or activities as well.

Organizational diagrams have several uses. They appear commonly in the form of a "family tree"—which is used not only to map family ancestry but also to plot the often complex historical process of business mergers and acquisitions. The "organogram" shows the inherent structure of an organization.

Other types of organizational diagrams include the flow chart (used to illustrate one or more flow patterns) and the diagnostic chart, a variation of the flow chart that shows alternative "routes" decided by the answers to questions embedded in the diagram.

Right Organizational diagrams link units of information. The units are usually shown contained in boxes, with some form of line connecting selected units. Weight of line and style of box can be varied in order to indicate different relationships.

Right and below You can vary the style of box to show status differences within the structure, and use different line weights, colors, and styles to indicate different types of relationships.

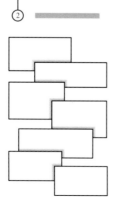

Right In flow charts, arrows indicate the path to be followed. In diagnostic charts, such as this, the route varies according to the condition that is determined following each question. You will frequently need to make several drafts in order to achieve a satisfactory design.

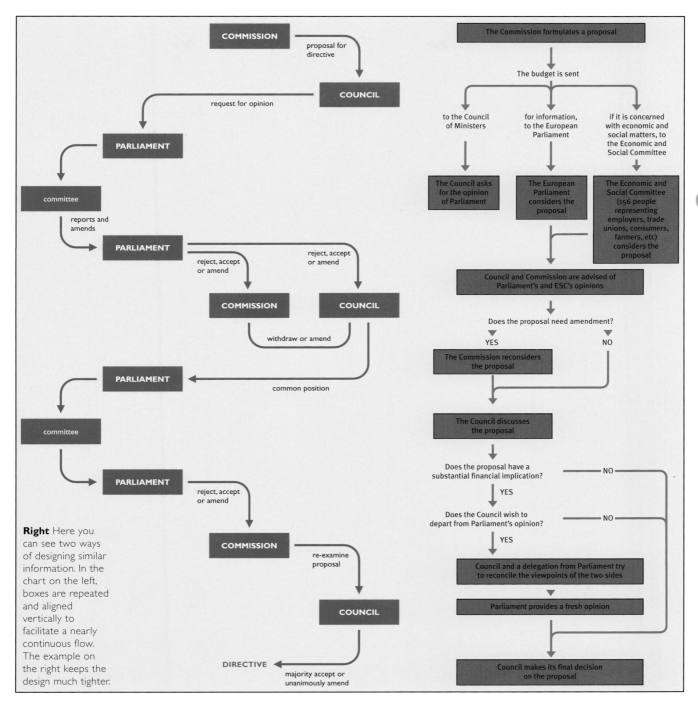

COMMISSION

proposal for directive

COUNCIL

request for opinion

PARLIAMENT

committee

reports and amends

PARLIAMENT

reject, accept or amend

reject, accept or amend

COMMISSION

COUNCIL

withdraw or amend

PARLIAMENT

common position

committee

PARLIAMENT

reject, accept or amend

COMMISSION

re-examine proposal

COUNCIL

DIRECTIVE

majority accept or unanimously amend

Right Here you can see two ways of designing similar information. In the chart on the left, boxes are repeated and aligned vertically to facilitate a nearly continuous flow. The example on the right keeps the design much tighter.

The Commission formulates a proposal

The budget is sent

to the Council of Ministers

for information, to the European Parliament

if it is concerned with economic and social matters, to the Economic and Social Committee

The Council asks for the opinion of Parliament

The European Parliament considers the proposal

The Economic and Social Committee (156 people representing employers, trade unions, consumers, farmers, etc) considers the proposal

Council and Commission are advised of Parliament's and ESC's opinions

Does the proposal need amendment?

YES   NO

The Commission reconsiders the proposal

The Council discusses the proposal

Does the proposal have a substantial financial implication?   NO

YES

Does the Council wish to depart from Parliament's opinion?   NO

YES

Council and a delegation from Parliament try to reconcile the viewpoints of the two sides

Parliament provides a fresh opinion

Council makes its final decision on the proposal

ORGANIZATIONAL DIAGRAMS 2

Right This "family tree" chart is used to show how corporations have grown by mergers and takeovers. The boxes are positioned vertically in a chronological order, which, given the space constraints, can be only relative.

Right This family tree is an organizational chart turned at a 90° angle and stripped of the usual boxes. With so many names to fit into a tight area, the names within each generation have been made into vertical lists, which take up less space. Leaving off the boxes also saves space. Bolding the names of direct descendants helps the reader to "navigate" through the chart.

RAIR Black Box

RAIR
SuperMicro
Turbo 386

RAIR
SuperMicro
Turbo 286

ARCNET

RAIR
PC workstation

IBM PC

Left Icons and pictograms not only add visual appeal but also aid understanding of organizational charts.

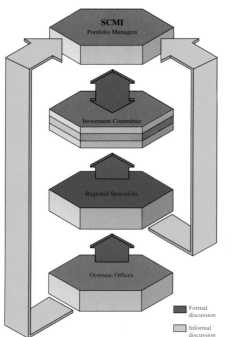

SCMI
Portfolio Managers

Investment Committee

Regional Specialists

Overseas Offices

Formal
discussion

Informal
discussion

Left Unusual shapes shown in 3-D add interest to what would otherwise be a very basic chart.

Right This diagram, showing values of imports and exports, uses the width of the arrows to display the quantities.

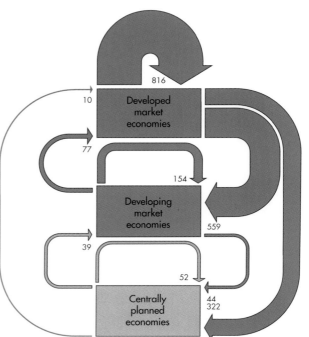

816

10

Developed
market
economies

77

154

Developing
market
economies

559

39

52

44
322

Centrally
planned
economies

ORGANIZATIONAL DIAGRAMS 3

Right In some cases you might want to avoid a hierarchical structure for an organizational chart. This "organogram" sites the head at the center, with the lines of management communication radiating out to the subsidiary divisions.

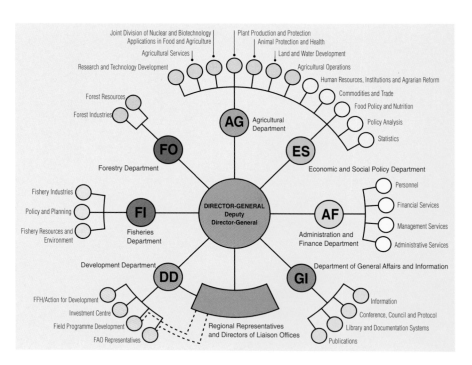

Right Add interest to an organizational diagram by drawing it at an angle.

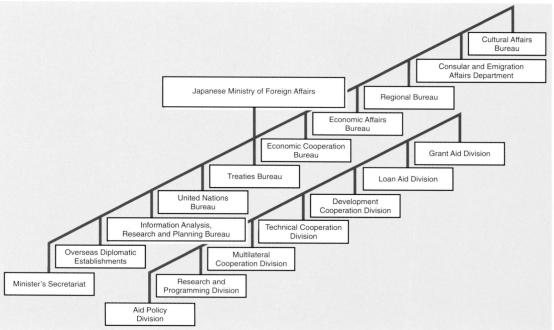

Right You can reduce some flow charts to a relatively simple structure of arrows and text—which excludes unnecessary visual clutter.

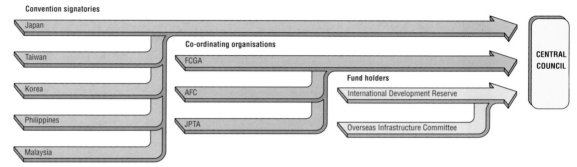

Below This cyclical flow diagram shows the physical relationship of the elements. It is designed to serve both as an aid to understanding and as a decorative style treatment.

Right Incorporating icons or pictograms in a chart not only adds interest but can be an effective way of saving space, especially when long scientific names would otherwise have to be included—and repeated.

113

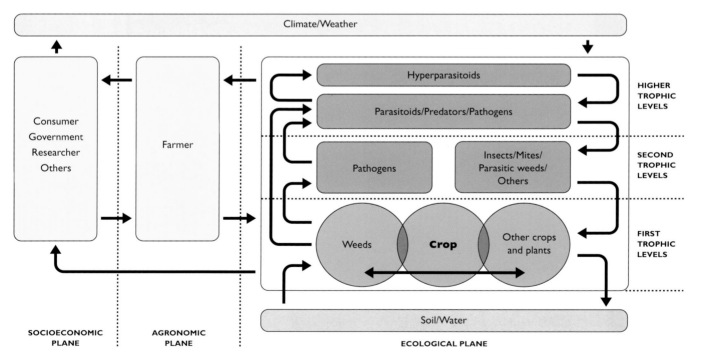

TIME DIAGRAMS 1

Organizing the presentation of time in tables or charts has its own particular problems. However, as with any other kind of information graphics, intelligent and sensitive design control will produce an invaluable tool for the reader that will allow the uninterrupted assimilation of information.

Apart from straightforward calendars or almanacs, time charts need to include variable, and often substantial, amounts of type matter. This may create problems when a time scale of equal division is required. Even when divisions can be varied, events involving substantial verbiage are unlikely to occur conveniently side-by-side. In such cases, skillful design is needed to ensure that the facts are displayed clearly in an easily understood chronological matrix.

114

Right There are special types of tables that have their own design considerations. A TV schedule can be made to function as an easy-to-read listing by arranging the column entries chronologically. The graphic clock device enables the user to find desired viewing times by quickly scanning down the left-hand column, while horizontal rules group program start times within each hourly period.

	1	2
🕐	▮▮▮ ▮▮▮▮▮▮▮▮▮▮▮ / ▮▮▮▮▮▮▮▮▮▮ / ▮▮▮▮▮▮▮▮ / ▮▮▮▮▮ / ▮▮▮ ▮▮▮▮▮▮▮▮▮▮ / ▮▮▮▮▮▮▮▮▮▮	▮▮▮ ▮▮▮▮▮▮▮▮▮▮▮ / ▮▮▮▮▮▮▮▮▮▮ / ▮▮▮ ▮▮▮▮▮▮▮▮▮▮
🕑	▮▮▮ ▮▮▮▮▮▮▮▮▮ / ▮▮▮▮▮▮▮▮▮ / ▮▮▮▮▮▮▮▮▮▮ / ▮▮▮▮▮	▮▮▮ ▮▮▮▮▮▮▮▮▮▮ / ▮▮▮▮▮▮▮▮▮▮ / ▮▮▮ ▮▮▮▮▮▮▮▮ / ▮▮▮▮▮▮▮ / ▮▮▮▮▮
🕒	▮▮▮ ▮▮▮▮ / ▮▮▮ ▮▮▮▮▮▮▮▮ / ▮▮▮▮▮ / ▮▮▮ ▮▮▮▮▮▮▮▮▮ / ▮▮▮▮▮▮▮▮▮ / ▮▮▮▮▮▮▮▮ / ▮▮▮▮▮▮▮	▮▮▮ ▮▮▮▮▮▮▮▮ / ▮▮▮ ▮▮▮▮▮▮▮▮▮ / ▮▮▮▮▮▮ / ▮▮▮▮▮
🕓	(continued)	▮▮▮ ▮▮▮▮▮▮▮▮▮▮
🕔		▮▮▮ ▮▮▮▮▮▮▮▮▮▮ / ▮▮▮▮▮▮▮▮ / ▮▮▮▮▮▮ / ▮▮▮ ▮▮▮▮▮▮▮▮▮▮
🕕	▮▮▮ ▮▮▮▮▮▮▮▮▮ / ▮▮▮▮▮▮▮▮ / ▮▮▮▮▮▮▮▮▮	▮▮▮ ▮▮▮▮▮▮▮▮▮▮ / ▮▮▮ ▮▮▮▮▮▮▮▮▮▮ / ▮▮▮ ▮▮▮▮▮▮▮▮▮
🕖	▮▮▮ ▮▮▮▮▮▮▮▮▮	▮▮▮ ▮▮▮▮▮▮▮▮▮▮ / ▮▮▮▮▮▮▮▮ / ▮▮▮▮▮▮ / ▮▮▮▮▮▮▮
🕗		▮▮▮ ▮▮▮▮▮▮▮▮▮▮

Transport timetables may include routes that have nonstop variations. Usually departure and arrival times are in chronological order, but this means sometimes lists will cross over. The convention is to break the list that is overlapped. A simple graphic enhancement like this soft shadow appears to "lift" the overlapping, express route. This has the joint effect of drawing attention to the limited-stop service and making the link to the split list easier to visualize. A more elaborate graphic treatment shows the route as linked circles but leaves open circles for the express route. The line for the slower service remains continuous, and so simpler to comprehend.

Moston	09.06	09.36	09.21	
Kirbeck	09.11	09.41		
Perton	09.21	09.51		
Suskwell	09.27	09.57		
Ormby	09.31	10.01 ▶		▶10.01
Newdyke	09.34		09.50	10.04
Kilbyton	09.38			10.08
Irborough	09.41			10.11
Ulanwood	09.46			10.16
Chitern	09.54			10.24
Klackford	10.10		09.58	10.40

Moston	09.06	09.36	09.21	
Kirbeck	09.11	09.41		
Perton	09.21	09.51		
Suskwell	09.27	09.57		
Ormby	09.31	10.01 ▲		
Newdyke	09.34		09.50	▲10.04
Kilbyton	09.38			10.08
Irborough	09.41			10.11
Ulanwood	09.46			10.16
Chitern	09.54			10.24
Klackford	10.10		09.58	10.40

Moston	●09.06	●09.36	●09.21	
Kirbeck	●09.11	●09.41	○	
Perton	●09.21	●09.51	○	
Suskwell	●09.27	●09.57	○	
Ormby	●09.31	●10.01	○	
Newdyke	●09.34		●09.50	●10.04
Kilbyton	●09.38		○	●10.08
Irborough	●09.41		○	●10.11
Ulanwood	●09.46		○	●10.16
Chitern	●09.54		○	●10.24
Klackford	●10.10		●09.58	●10.40

Right Apply a little imagination and a few simple graphics, and what might have been a boring listing of information can be transformed into a useful and interesting design.

115

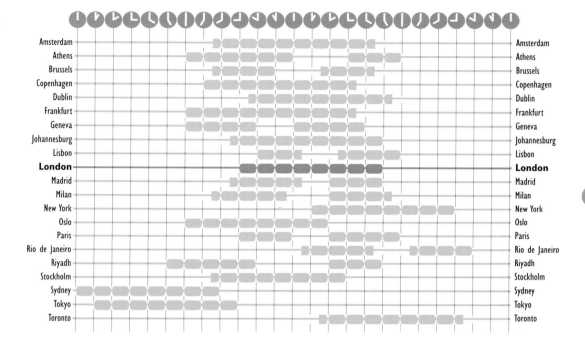

	Amsterdam		Amsterdam
	Athens		Athens
	Brussels		Brussels
	Copenhagen		Copenhagen
	Dublin		Dublin
	Frankfurt		Frankfurt
	Geneva		Geneva
	Johannesburg		Johannesburg
	Lisbon		Lisbon
	London		**London**
	Madrid		Madrid
	Milan		Milan
	New York		New York
	Oslo		Oslo
	Paris		Paris
	Rio de Janeiro		Rio de Janeiro
	Riyadh		Riyadh
	Stockholm		Stockholm
	Sydney		Sydney
	Tokyo		Tokyo
	Toronto		Toronto

You can turn a simple but repetitive list of dates into an attractive visual image. Again, all you need is a little imagination and a few graphic tricks.

Right These two examples show how you can indicate time durations using the clockface symbol. The first illustrates the time accumulation, the time of the current action being highlighted. In the second example, the arrow emphasizes the dynamic progress.

TIME DIAGRAMS 2

Right Cyclical time patterns often can be plotted as circular charts. This chart combines several related elements of information. The repetitious nature of the menstrual process is made particularly clear by the continuity of the circle.

116

 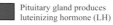

Menstrual period Pituitary gland produces follicle-stimulating hormone (FSH) Pituitary gland produces luteinizing hormone (LH)

Below Another useful visual device that can be employed in time-chart design is the calendar block. This creates a focus for the particular date, or it can be the commencement point for a month or year.

Below You can plot timelines vertically or horizontally. Shown below is an example of a vertical time chart in which the entries are also offset along a horizontal relative timescale.

Below If entries vary in proximity and line length, use leader lines to relate the points to an exact position along the time scale. This should give you room to accommodate longer entries with enough separation to ensure legibility.

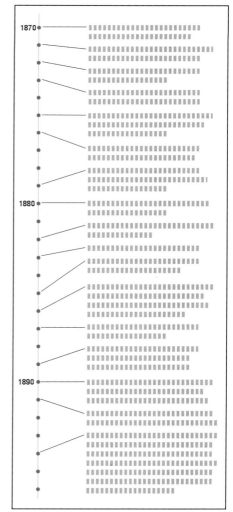

117

TIME DIAGRAMS 3

Right As time is usually perceived as a linear progression, timelines are often plotted to read from left to right. This makes it difficult to fit long entries. Offset them vertically, and use a bullet device to align the points visually to the time scale.

Right Alternatively, you can run the scale through the middle of the chart area and use angled type to accommodate the line entries.

Right Timelines may need to cover long durations. Simple perspective enables you to compress the timeline. It also allows more space for fitting text elements relating to recent events.

118

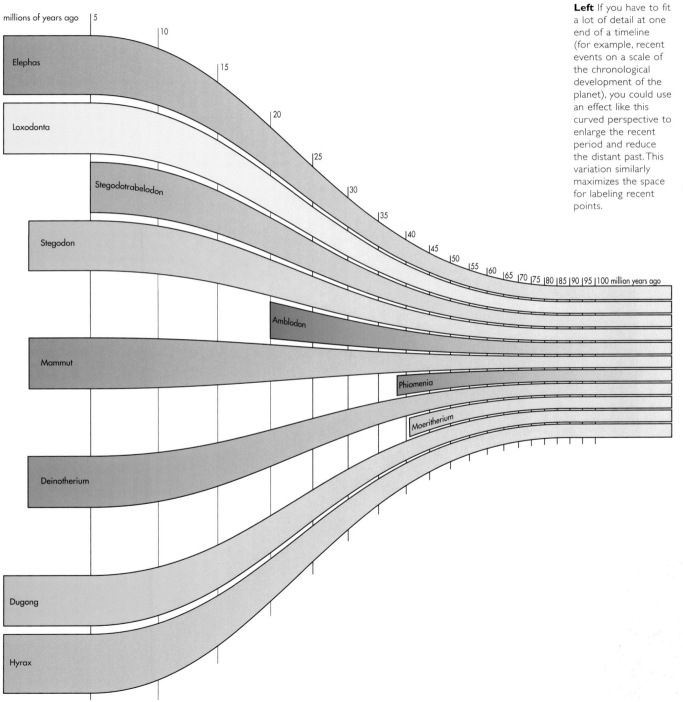

millions of years ago |5

|10

|15

|20

|25

|30

|35

|40

|45

|50

|55

|60

|65 |70 |75 |80 |85 |90 |95 |100 million years ago

Elephas

Loxodonta

Stegodotrabelodon

Stegodon

Amblodon

Mammut

Phiomenia

Moeritherium

Deinotherium

Dugong

Hyrax

Left If you have to fit a lot of detail at one end of a timeline (for example, recent events on a scale of the chronological development of the planet), you could use an effect like this curved perspective to enlarge the recent period and reduce the distant past. This variation similarly maximizes the space for labeling recent points.

Below Using a Bézier drawing tool, you can draw a filled graph. Make a thin round-cornered box and adjust its angle, by trial and error, to match a segment of the graph line. Duplicate the box and adjust the angle to create the graph line as a broad rule.

You can then duplicate and offset the line to create a shadow. You can also create a shadow for the grid.

Below To produce a single-line graph, you'll have to draw each of the line segments individually, and the ends probably won't abut nicely. Use small point markers to disguise this *(top)*, or make a feature of the point markers *(center)*. These balls are

simply circular boxes with a graduated fill and a small highlight. Alternatively, having drawn the Bézier outline, you could create a series of parallel vertical lines and extend these to align their tops with the graph line *(bottom)*.

PAGE LAYOUT SOFTWARE 2

Below Simple filled boxes created with a page layout program make basic bar charts. Use graduated tints of colors to produce more striking effects. To make shadow effects, duplicate the bars, then change the colors to gray and position them behind.

Below Each of these metallic-looking bars is made of four bars. Two are abutting. One has a graduated fill of cyan to black; below it is a black to yellow-brown bar. A thin white filled bar makes the highlight, and all are contained within a black outline. The cigarettes are produced in much the same way—with the addition of the glowing end. The stamped envelopes are three rectangles, one with rounded corners. These are grouped and turned 25°, then duplicated to create the required number.

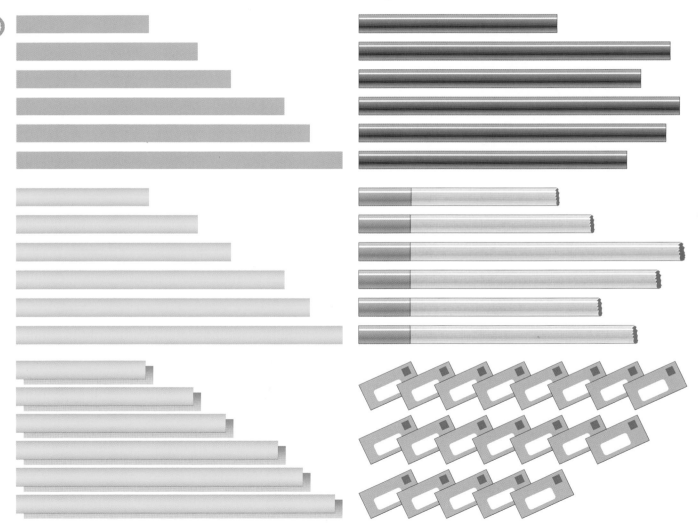

Below These gold ingots are made up of four rectangles, the top face having a blended fill. The certificates consist of a blended fill, plus a circle of red and some gray lines. These are grouped and angled. Vary the angle to make a more interesting shape.

Below Spherical beads are also simple to create, by using a circular box with a circular blended fill and adding a small white highlight. Each of the 3-D bars is a straightforward rectangle, with two skewed rectangles to form the end and underside.

You can manufacture a line of cubes in the same way, adjusting the width of the last cube to create the fraction.

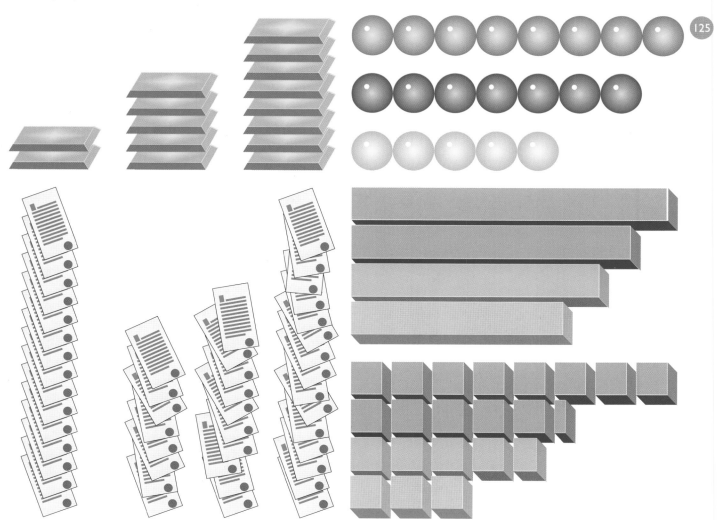

125

PAGE LAYOUT SOFTWARE 3

Below Square area charts are easy to construct within page layout programs. Calculate the square root of the value of each item and use this to draw square boxes to the required size. You may then want to resize the boxes as a group to suit your layout.

Below Circular area charts are slightly more complicated. The area of a circle is πr^2 (3.142 × the square of the radius). Divide the value by 3.142 and then find the square root of that figure. This gives you the size of the radius. Double this to obtain the diameter of the circle. Once you've drawn all of the circles you'll probably have to enlarge or reduce them as a group to fit the layout.

Below Unit area charts are even easier to produce. Start with the greatest value and just draw a suitably sized shape, then step and repeat to the required number for each value.

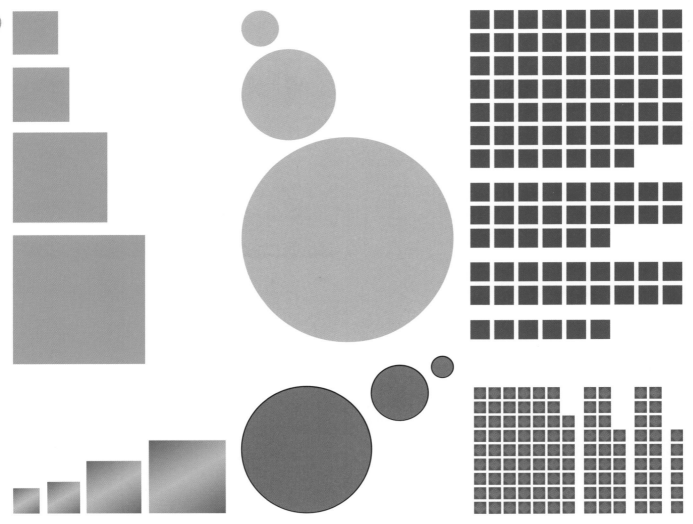

Below Construct a pie chart by drawing a circular box (*1*). Draw a horizontal box from the center to the edge of the circle. The height of this box should be set to the line width you want (*2*). Take the percentage value of the first segment and multiply it by 3.6 to convert it to degrees. Set the rotation of the new box to that angle (*3*), then move the box so it radiates from the center of the circle (*4*). Clone the first box again and rotate this by the sum of the first and second segment values (in degrees) (*5*). Next, position this box (*6*), then repeat for all other segments (*7*) except the last (the box for which would be identical to the first). Set the circular box color and line box colors as you want them (*8*). To add color to the segments you will need to use a drawing tool to trace over the segment lines. Be sure to extend the segment color beyond the edge of the circle (*9*). Repeat this, setting the fill color for each segment (*10*). Arrange the layering of the elements so that the segment-dividing lines are in front (*11*). Finally, duplicate the base circle. Keep it concentric, but extend the diameter so that it encloses all overlapping segment color boxes. Delete the fill and add a frame of the page color that is wide enough to clean up the uneven edges (*12*).

127

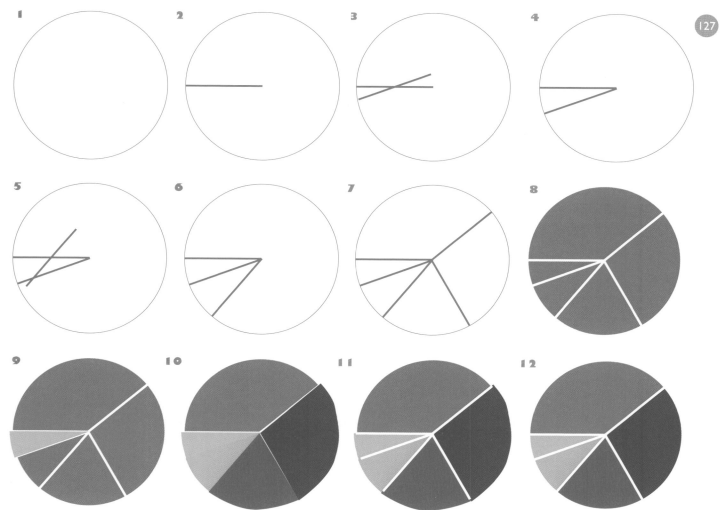

PAGE LAYOUT SOFTWARE 4

Below You can create the 3-D blocks for organizational diagrams in the same way as 3-D bars. The red dotted lines are simply duplicated circles, as are the drop shadows. Below is a much more subtle treatment, which shows the boxes as embossed plaques.

Below By using a metallic effect, you can give shapes and lines a high-tech look. There are just two boxes for each block, each with a graduated tint. Angled white lines separate the sides to make them look like edges.

Below Convincing spheres, floating above soft shadows, are simple to construct using graduated tints in circular boxes. The shadows are pale shades of gray blended to white.

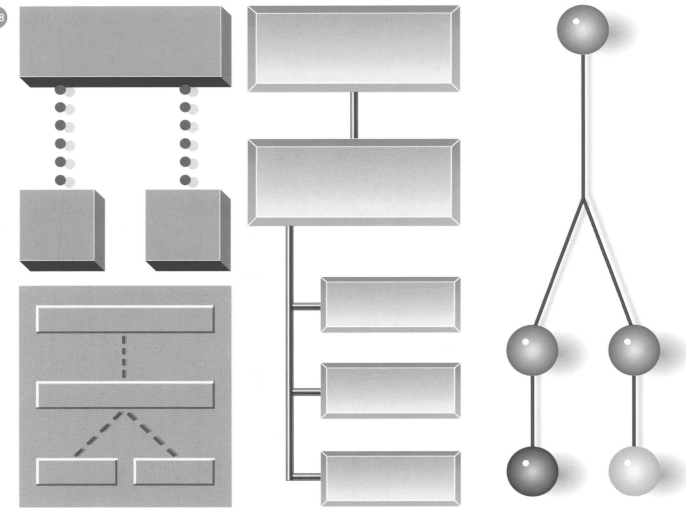

Below You can even
create effective maps
using a page layout
program. First, import
a base map of the
required area (a clip-
art map would do).
Then create a matrix
of suitably sized small
squares or circles to
cover the map area.
Delete any shapes
that fall outside the
map area, and color
those within it as
appropriate. The
result can be a highly
effective graphic.
It is also possible, with
sufficient memory
allocated to software,
to create a map from
spherical-bead shapes
without leaving your
page layout program.

129

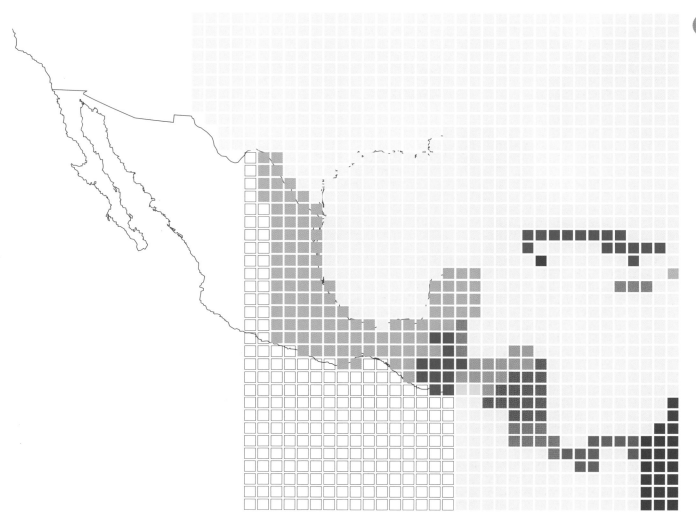

VECTOR SOFTWARE 1

Undoubtedly, the vector drawing program is the information designer's key tool. Although you can achieve a great deal with a page layout program and raster painting software, the vector drawing program has been specifically designed to suit the purposes of the graphic designer. A good professional vector program provides minute control combined with a wide range of creative options.

Below left Keep corners of angled boxes tidy by setting the join to either a rounded or a chamfered mitre. Graph lines with acute angles will also benefit from rounding or chamfering.

Below When you're drawing 3-D boxes, the easiest way to get precision at the corners is to clone the first rectangle (that is, duplicate it in the same position), then ungroup the clone and drag the upper corners to the desired position. Simply clone this shape and drag the side corners till they "snap" to the corners of the original rectangle.

Below Tools like the step-and-repeat facility speed up the diagram-making process. Draw one bar to the proportion you want, then step-and-repeat. Make bar charts by using data values for the box widths, then resize the whole chart to fit the space available.

Below It is possible to create an almost limitless range of line styles with vector drawing software. Multiple graduated fills produce good effects. Try blending cloned lines that are styled differently. Draw oversized wavy lines, then reduce them to produce tight curves. Soft shadows are easily produced by offsetting cloned shapes and filling them with blends from dark to base color—include the elements of the base color in the dark shadow specification.

VECTOR SOFTWARE 2

Below Embossed or engraved effects are also easy to produce. The convention is to assume a virtual light source at top left, but don't let that hinder creativity. So long as the chart is readable, you can be as wild as you like.

Below Geometric shapes are simple to create and can be given a convincing 3-D quality with a little careful filling and shadowing. Circles with offset graduated fills will look a bit flat. To make spheres, superimpose two circles with blended fills. Follow the steps

below. Draw a base circle with no line and a light fill. Add a smaller second circle, offset and with a dark fill. Clone it and blend the original of these with the base circle. Now draw a small circle with a light fill and blend this with the second of the mid circles. This technique

works with other shapes, too. You can pick up the top shape and move it to adjust the effect.

Below Use facilities such as joining filled paths to create "holes" through which a graduated fill or some other complex fill needs to be seen. This is also handy for lake areas in maps.

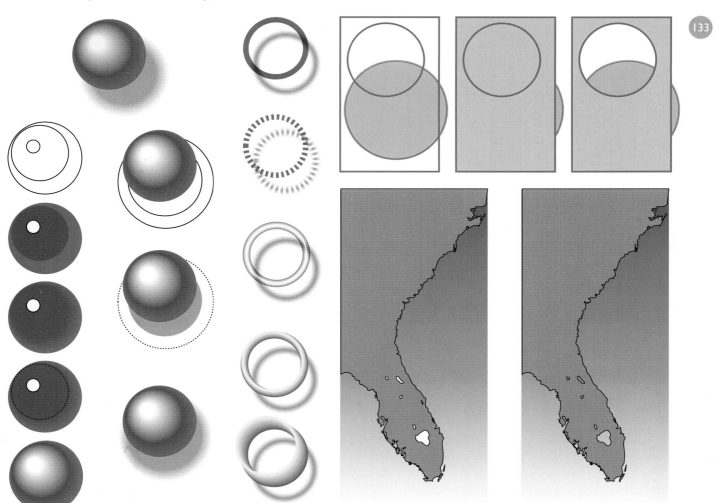

RASTER SOFTWARE

Although they are largely used for modifying or enhancing vector-generated diagrams, it is possible to create charts directly in raster paint programs. You will need to be able to draw shapes and adjust their dimensions, preferably by keying in values rather than by manual manipulation. You will also need to be able to reposition items accurately. But any current version of a raster-based painting program should facilitate that. You can of course create a base vector image using a page layout or drawing program and import that into the paint program (provided the import has a good level of resolution). The major advantage of using the raster program is in the range of image manipulation features you can use. Photographic images can be used as bases, as they are or with any number of filtered effects, and diagrams can be created from these bases.

134

Below A color image serves as the base for this chart. The columns are made by setting the selection tool to the size required. Start by making vertical guides at measured intervals across the image and then set a base line (you'll have to invert the image if the selection tool selects from the top down). Make the tallest bar first. Note the pixel height and use this as a conversion factor for all the other values in the chart. Reset the selection tool for each column. Once you have all the columns selected you can modify them—by adding an outline, or adjusting the contrast or the color choice. If you then select the rest of the image you will also be able to manipulate that.

Below Using the same base a simple graph can be drawn. Use guides to align and draw the grid. The point marker is created and copied. Then each one is located by reference to the grid and a line is drawn to connect the point markers.

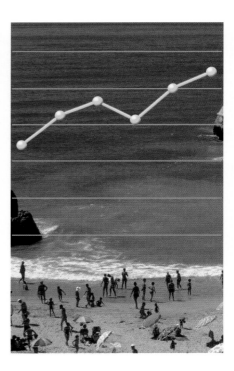

Below This column chart was produced simply by cropping a suitable image to the required width and then scaling the part above the runner's head to the required height. Any distortion is immaterial given the blurriness of the background.

Below Pie charts can be constructed from suitable images. Crop the circular shape, then draw a line for one side of the first segment. Duplicate the line and rotate it to the degree value required (percentage value × 3.6°). Repeat for the other segment lines. You can then add a soft shadow to highlight a segment. Or you can select and move the segments to make an exploded pie chart.

Below Like the bar chart examples on the facing page, this flow chart was made by selecting areas and then adjusting the brightness and contrast settings. Frames were added to the selections and the connecting lines made by filling selected areas.

135

3-D SOFTWARE 1

Yyou are probably most familiar with those industry-standard applications best suited for producing your day-to-day work, such as page layout, drawing, image manipulation, and Web design. A 3-D application will probably not form part of your graphic armory, not least because of the steep learning curve required to use one. However, even a basic 3-D application can provide a fast way of creating very effective diagram art, with only a minimal amount of knowledge.

1 | 2 | 3
3-D applications provide tools for generating simple block diagrams in a matter of minutes. This diagram (1, 2) took just ten minutes to construct and render. Size fields allow you to enter accurate dimensions (3).

4 | 5 | 6 | 7 | 8
One immediate advantage of using a 3-D application is that it allows you to quickly rotate an image or alter the perspective to suit particular situations, such as fitting a layout or emphasizing (or disguising!) a statistic.

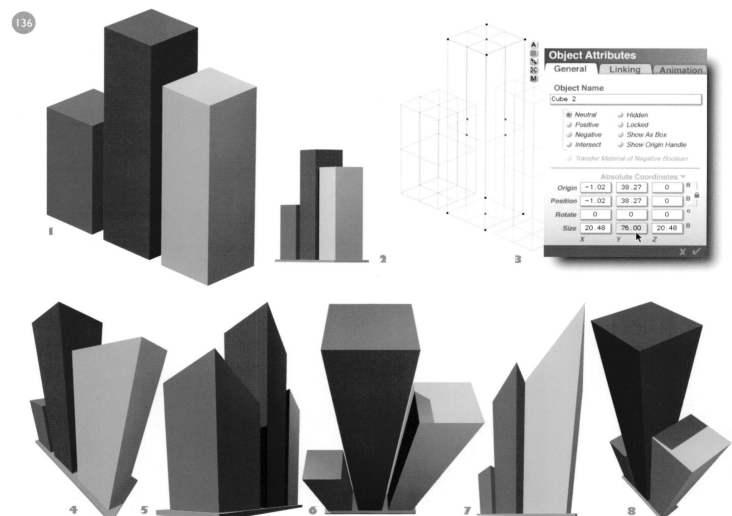

1 | 2 | 3
Most 3-D applications come with rendering tools that allow you to apply a variety of effects, such as plain color (*1*), solid (*2*), or transparent (*3*) characteristics, which you can either define yourself or choose from a built-in "gallery" of effects.

4 | 5 | 6 | 7
As well as being given any one of a variety of surface effects, objects can be molded into any basic shape. These shapes can be modified, such as this cylinder (*4*), which is shown as a tube (*5*), stacked tubes (*6*), and tubes within tubes (*7*).

137

1

2

3

4

5

6

7

3-D SOFTWARE 2

1 | 2

Although simple techniques can be used to good effect, such as nesting one object within another (1) to give comparisons of volume, more dramatic results can be achieved by separating out the objects (2).

3

Built-in rendering features give effective graphic results as in example (2), but another technique that is often more appropriate is to use 3-D "mapping" features to wrap pictures around objects (3).

4 | 5 | 6

The technique of making an indentation in a solid object is known as a "Boolean" operation, which means, in effect, subtracting one object from another. In the example (2), this was achieved by duplicating the cube and then resizing it to the appropriate dimensions (4). The smaller cube was then given a "negative" attribute while the larger one retained its "positive" one. This operation resulted in removing the smaller cube from the larger one, the inside walls retaining all of the surface and lighting characteristics that had already been set for the larger cube (5). Finally, a new cube with a different surface texture was added to the scene, which gave it the appearance of hovering above the larger cube (6, shown straight on).

138

1

2

3

4

5

6

1 | 2
Although 3-D applications provide features for modeling an object out of almost any kind of material, rendering time becomes an important issue for complex objects. The criteria which affect rendering time are effects such as refraction, reflection, and transparency— the more you apply of each the longer a scene takes to render. The glass discs in the pie diagram (1) use high settings of all three attributes and consequently took around twelve hours to render at this size—even on a fast computer! Diagram (2) uses the same discs as (1) but with simpler textures applied, and thus was rendered in a matter of minutes rather than hours.

3
Another advantage of 3-D rendering applications is that they provide an effective way of departing from conventional methods of representing values, as shown here with these glass balls of varying sizes.

139

2

1

3

READY-MADE RESOURCES

Ready-made graphic resources in the form of clip-art collections, royalty-free photographs, and backgrounds abound, with a quality of image ranging from high-end professional (at high-end cost) to unusable—and all too often the latter. If you are a professional graphic designer you may scorn the idea of such ready-made resources on the basis that their accessibility runs contrary to the ethos of your profession —after all, you're being paid to provide originality, not merely to regurgitate the same material that anyone can use. However, image resources need not be viewed as competition for your imagination, but as an extension to it, particularly if it provides a cost-effective means of incorporating otherwise costly images into your graphics.

Perhaps the most valuable resources are high-end mapping resources such as Cartesia's Map Art and Digital Wisdom's Mountain High Maps, the latter of which was used to illustrate these pages. Generating accurate maps can be a costly and time-consuming business, often getting in the way of your creative flow, not to mention deadlines. These resources generally come in the form of a "kit" of separate parts (e.g., topographic relief, coastlines, rivers, and country borders), which not only allows you to select just the elements that you need for the job, but to use the drawing or image-manipulation applications with which you are already familiar. The rest is up to your imagination.

Below Mapping resources generally come as a "kit" of separate parts, provided as separate layers or individual components in industry-standard file formats, thus allowing you to use the software packages with which you are most familiar. The examples below were generated in Adobe Photoshop, using "alpha channels" for land and sea masks, and "paths" for rivers and state borders. The wide variety of effects were applied simply by playing with image adjustment controls and shadow effects.

Grundy & Northedge
Heading icons for
Bloomberg magazine.
Created with Adobe
Illustrator. Unusually
detailed icons covering
a wide range of
complex activities.
The underlying grid
structure and consistent
graphic treatment
unifies what might
otherwise be a
disparate collection
of shapes and styles.

Strategies

Web watch

Tuned in

Toolbox

Signals

What's working

Books

That was then

Getting technical

Grundy & Northedge
Icons for the Camelot
annual report (designed
by the MPL design
group). Created using
Adobe Illustrator.
In this series color
is used to hold icon
groupings in their
relevant categories.

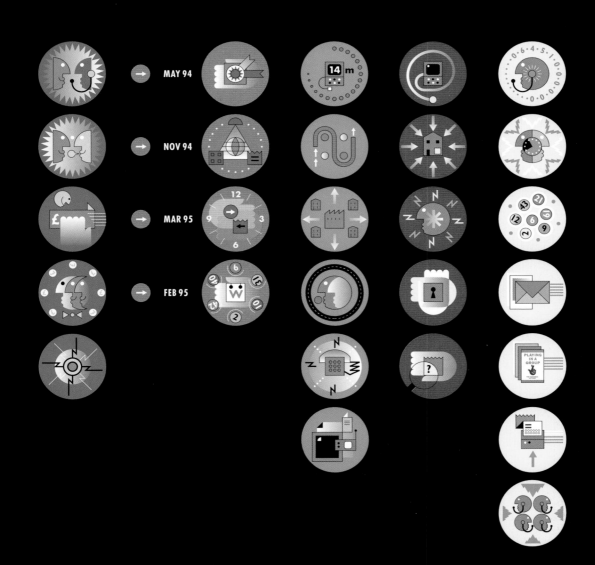

MAY 94

NOV 94

MAR 95

FEB 95

Nigel Holmes
Illustration showing
readers how to
carry out a breast
examination, created
for *Self* magazine
using Macromedia
FreeHand. The human
figure is reduced to
a simple, stylized
outline.

Annabel Milne
How to clean your teeth. Created for demonstration purposes using Adobe Illustrator. This realistic styling of the human form still succeeds in keeping detail to a minimum. The sequence shows line and tone methods varying from monochrome with line and flat tint through to simple color rendering.

147

Nigel Holmes
Illustration of Greg
Louganis's reverse
two-and-a-half-pike
dive, created for
Olympic Dreams
(published by Rizzoli)
using Macromedia
FreeHand. A complex
physical action clearly
shown in a simple
sillhouette sequence.

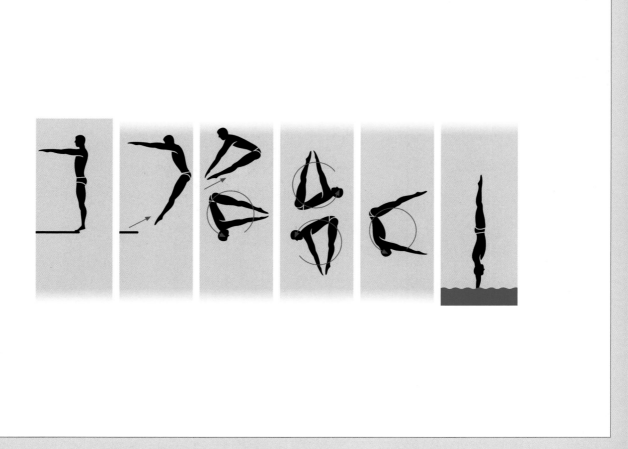

Annabel Milne
Angiogenesis, showing payloaded antibodies targeting cancer cells. Created for Antisoma plc prospectus, using Adobe Illustrator and Adobe Dimensions. The exaggerated perspective view and bright colors on a black base give the diagram a dramatic space-fantasy feel. The various items cannot, of course, be drawn realistically but instead have an almost mechanical styling, which also contributes to the overall effect.

© A.Milne 1999

Nigel Holmes
Map of the parts of the brain, created for a medical magazine published by *Time*, using Macromedia FreeHand. This highly stylized modular treatment uses colored type to identify and describe the component parts.

Although created with a vector drawing program, a treatment like this could be achieved with page layout software.

150

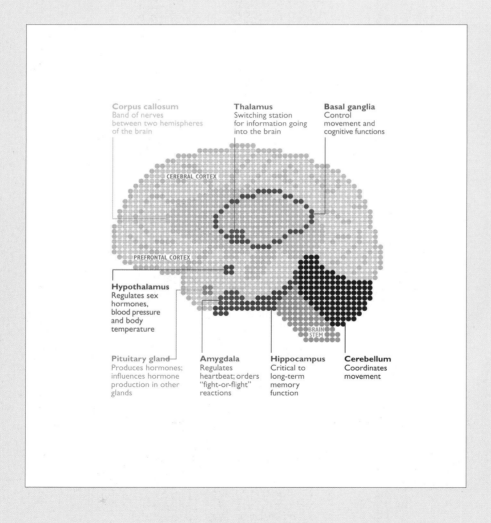

Corpus callosum
Band of nerves between two hemispheres of the brain

Thalamus
Switching station for information going into the brain

Basal ganglia
Control movement and cognitive functions

CEREBRAL CORTEX

PREFRONTAL CORTEX

Hypothalamus
Regulates sex hormones, blood pressure and body temperature

BRAIN STEM

Pituitary gland
Produces hormones; influences hormone production in other glands

Amygdala
Regulates heartbeat; orders "fight-or-flight" reactions

Hippocampus
Critical to long-term memory function

Cerebellum
Coordinates movement

John Grimwade
Round-the-world
balloons, created for
Popular Science using
Adobe Illustrator.
Two different scales
are employed in this
illustrative diagram.
One is used to show
the comparative sizes
of the balloons, the
other for the cabins.
Each has a scale bar
but the second also
has the human
silhouettes that
help in establishing
a visual scale.

151

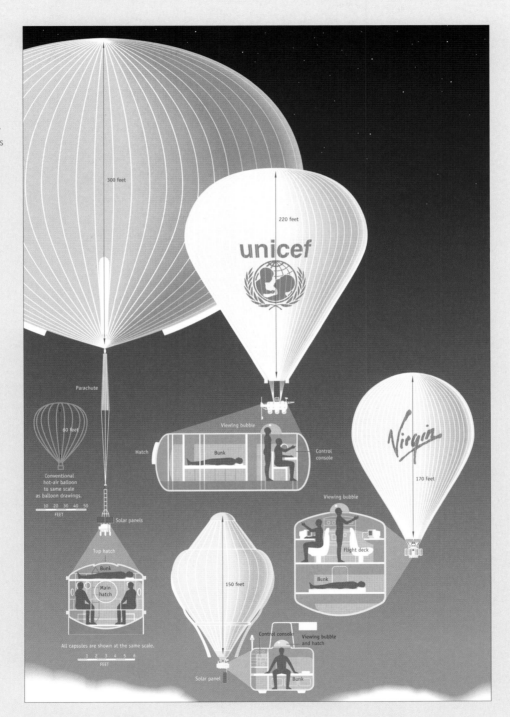

300 feet

220 feet

unicef

Parachute

60 feet

Viewing bubble

Hatch   Bunk   Control console

Virgin

170 feet

Conventional
hot-air balloon
to same scale
as balloon drawings.

10 20 30 40 50
FEET

Solar panels

Viewing bubble

Top hatch

Bunk

Main
hatch

Flight deck

Bunk

150 feet

All capsules are shown at the same scale.

1 2 3 4 5 6
FEET

Control console   Viewing bubble
and hatch

Solar panel   Bunk

Nigel Holmes
Illustration of the workings of a gas engine, created for *Attaché* magazine using Macromedia FreeHand. A clever combination of detailed technical representation with a cartoon treatment to lighten the effect.

Bill Le Bihan
The four-stroke combustion engine cycle (known affectionately as suck, squeeze, bang, puff), created for a partwork series using Macromedia FreeHand. This detailed diagram of the combustion process makes good use of the blend feature available in vector drawing software.

The Four Stroke Cycle

1

INLET VALVE OPEN   EXHAUST VALVE CLOSED

PISTON MOVES DOWN, DRAWING IN PETROL–AIR MIXTURE

2

INLET VALVE CLOSED   EXHAUST VALVE CLOSED

PISTON MOVES UP, TO COMPRESS PETROL–AIR MIXTURE

3

INLET VALVE CLOSED   EXHAUST VALVE CLOSED

PISTON MOVES DOWN, BY PRODUCTS OF COMBUSTION

4

INLET VALVE CLOSED   EXHAUST VALVE OPEN

PISTON MOVES UP, EXPELLING PRODUCTS OF COMBUSTION

John Grimwade
Illustration showing how a pipe organ works, created for *Smithsonian* magazine using Adobe Illustrator. Several diagrams are successfully combined here to illustrate a highly complex structure and process. In order to achieve this, many of the pipes are not shown and other elements are reduced to simple structures. Note the use of the human silhouette to aid appreciation of the scale of the pipes.

154

THE PIPES
Large organs have thousands of pipes ranging in length from a few inches to over thirty feet.

The smallest / The largest

Tuning wire

Upper lip
Mouth

Reed tongue

Lower lip

Shallot

REED PIPE

FLUE PIPE

Foot hole

Foot hole

Pipes

AIR

Foot hole

Key channel

Key channel
9

Slider

AIR

8

Pallet

Windchest

Link to key

6

4
Wind chest

HOW A MECHANICAL PIPE ORGAN WORKS

7 Keyboard

A blower 1 pushes air through a regulating valve into a reservoir 2 . From there air travels up the wind trunk 3 into an airtight box, the wind chest 4 . Rows, or ranks, of pipes are controlled by a stop knob. As the knob 5 is pulled out, a long strip of wood, called a slider 6 , is moved. It has holes that match the positions of the pipes. This opens the air pathway to a complete row of pipes. When the organist presses a key 7 , a valve or pallet 8 opens, and lets air reach the key channel 9 . This allows all pipes on that channel, for which stops have been opened, to produce sound.

Mechanical link

Mechanical link

Stop knob 5

3 Wind trunk

AIR

Regulating valve

2 Reservoir   AIR

1 Blower

John Grimwade
Cutaway diagram of New York's Grand Central Station, created for *Condé Nast Traveler* using Adobe Illustrator. Another highly complex structure edited to facilitate understanding by the lay reader. Floors are "floated" apart to reveal information. The human forms are used here again to indicate the scale of the structure.

42ND STREET

Tennis courts

5 Sky Ceiling
Patch left uncleaned

6

Skywalks

8 Chandeliers
Chandeliers

Campbell Apartment
One of three planned balcony restaurants

Oyster Bar ramp
7
Ticket windows
West Balcony
Escalators to MetLife Building

1 Entrance
Bridge over ramps

4
West Staircase
Upper train platforms

Information booth
East Balcony

Ramp
3 Main Concourse
Half-acre Tennessee marble floor
New East Staircase

2 Main Waiting Room

To Lexington Passage
To Grand Central Market and Lexington Avenue entrance
To Graybar Passage

Oyster Bar 10
9
Vaulted ceiling
Oyster Bar ramp
Ramp
11 Lower Concourse

New restaurants and bars

Lower train platforms

Nigel Holmes
Illustration explaining the size of the US national debt. Created for Richard Saul Wurman's book *Understanding USA* (TED Conferences Inc.), using Macromedia FreeHand. A series of charts and illustrations that serve as a visual analogy ("a drop in the ocean"). Despite the quirky treatment, the hard facts are illustrated with great clarity.

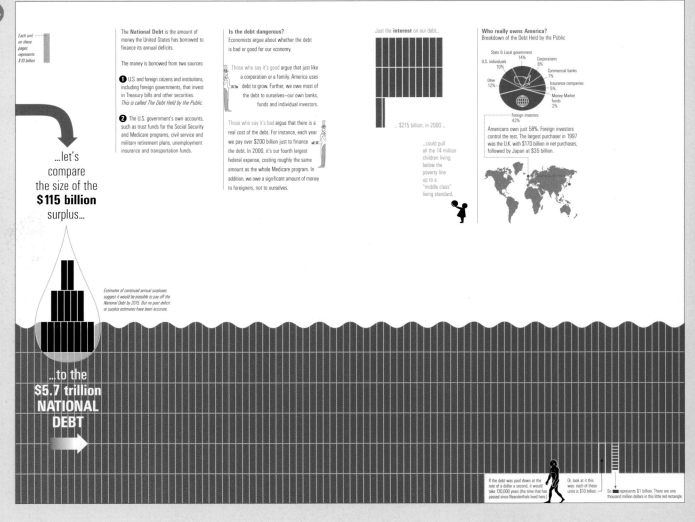

Each unit on these pages represents $10 billion

...let's compare the size of the **$115 billion** surplus...

Estimates of continued annual surpluses suggest it would be possible to pay off the National Debt by 2015. But no past deficit or surplus estimates have been accurate.

...to the **$5.7 trillion NATIONAL DEBT**

The **National Debt** is the amount of money the United States has borrowed to finance its annual deficits.

The money is borrowed from two sources:

❶ U.S. and foreign citizens and institutions, including foreign governments, that invest in Treasury bills and other securities. *This is called The Debt Held by the Public.*

❷ The U.S. government's own accounts, such as trust funds for the Social Security and Medicare programs, civil service and military retirement plans, unemployment insurance and transportation funds.

Is the debt dangerous?
Economists argue about whether the debt is bad or good for our economy.

Those who say it's good argue that just like a corporation or a family, America uses debt to grow. Further, we owe most of the debt to ourselves—our own banks, funds and individual investors.

Those who say it's bad argue that there is a real cost of the debt. For instance, each year we pay over $200 billion just to finance the debt. In 2000, it's our fourth largest federal expense, costing roughly the same amount as the whole Medicare program. In addition, we owe a significant amount of money to foreigners, not to ourselves.

Just the **interest** on our debt...

... $215 billion, in 2000 ...

...could pull all the 14 million children living below the poverty line up to a "middle class" living standard.

Who really owns America?
Breakdown of the Debt Held by the Public

State & Local government 14%
U.S. individuals 10%
Other 12%
Corporations 8%
Commercial banks 7%
Insurance companies 5%
Money Market funds 2%
Foreign investors 42%

Americans own just 58%. Foreign investors control the rest. The largest purchaser in 1997 was the U.K. with $170 billion in net purchases, followed by Japan at $35 billion.

If the debt was paid down at the rate of a dollar a second, it would take 130,000 years (the time that has passed since Neanderthals lived here.)

Or, look at it this way: each of these units is $10 billion.

So ▬ represents $1 billion. There are one thousand million dollars in this little red rectangle.

bounford.com
Statistical bar
chart created for
Worldlink magazine,
using Macromedia
FreeHand. The grid is
used here as a visual
benchmark with
excessive items
breaking out beyond
the general norm.
Even so there are
values too great to be
included in the scale
and these have to be
represented by the
"broken" bar.

Grundy & Northedge
Five financial crashes in history, created for *Worldlink* magazine using Adobe Illustrator. A light treatment using the visual analogy of bursting bubbles—the pin indicating the point in time when the bubbles burst.

158

4

1990 Japan

39,000

Nikkei Index

1978 1980 1982 1984 1986 1988 1990 1992 1994 1996 1998

1929 The Great Crash

381.7

198.69

41.22

1928 1929 1930 1931 1932

1999 Internet Stocks

5

Nasdaq Index

2,500

2,000

1,500

1,000

500

0

OCT 95   JULY 96   APR 97   JAN 98   OCT 98

bounford.com
Diagram showing the range of airport investment by BAA. Created using Macromedia FreeHand. Using the map base to locate the airports helps the reader see the regional allocation of investment.

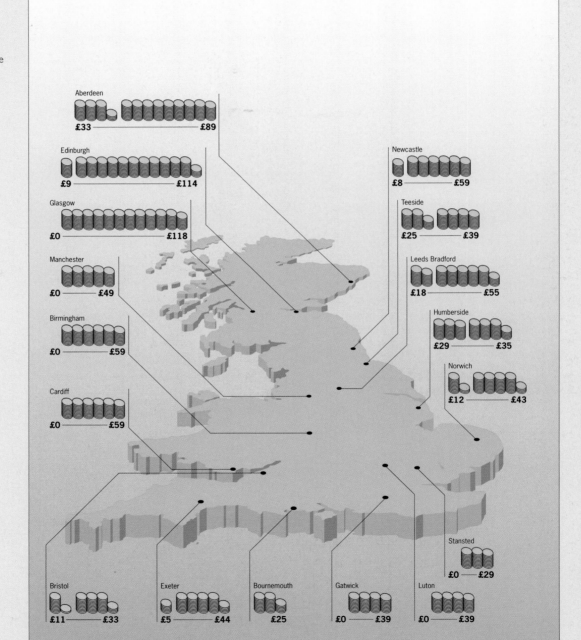

Aberdeen £33 — £89

Edinburgh £9 — £114

Glasgow £0 — £118

Manchester £0 — £49

Birmingham £0 — £59

Cardiff £0 — £59

Newcastle £8 — £59

Teeside £25 — £39

Leeds Bradford £18 — £55

Humberside £29 — £35

Norwich £12 — £43

Stansted £0 — £29

Bristol £11 — £33

Exeter £5 — £44

Bournemouth £25

Gatwick £0 — £39

Luton £0 — £39

bounford.com
Diagram showing the dumping of radioactive waste at sea by European countries, created for Greenpeace International using Macromedia FreeHand. A simple bar chart given drama by the illustrative "background." The use of perspective enhances the effect but a scale is included to make it possible to read the values accurately.

Year | 1967 1969 1971 1972 1973 1974 1975 1976 1977 1978 1979 1980 1981 1982

Radioactive Waste per 1,000 Curies

10
20
30
40
50
60
70
80
90
100
110
120
130
140
150
160
170
180
190

Key

Combined Waste:
Belgium
Netherlands
Switzerland
France
Italy
Germany
Sweden

UK Radioactive Waste

161

John Grimwade
Map showing the layout and location of Angkor Wat, created for *Condé Nast Traveler* using Adobe Illustrator. A simple street map drawn in perspective, which is enhanced by the atmospheric aerial perspective effect.

Salient buildings are shown as 3-D illustrations. The inset location map is drawn to the same perspective projection.

Nigel Holmes
The bombing of the Uffizi Museum in Florence, created for *Time* magazine using Macromedia FreeHand. In this news diagram, a relatively simple 3-D representation of the building is shown superimposed on the local street layout. Labels are kept away from the key structure and are located by arrows.

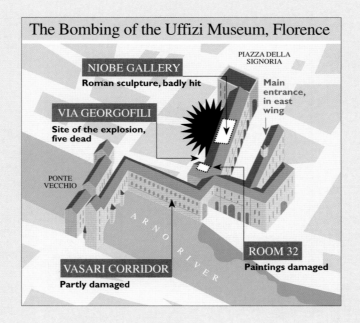

The Bombing of the Uffizi Museum, Florence

PIAZZA DELLA SIGNORIA

NIOBE GALLERY
Roman sculpture, badly hit

Main entrance, in east wing

VIA GEORGOFILI
Site of the explosion, five dead

PONTE VECCHIO

ARNO RIVER

ROOM 32
Paintings damaged

VASARI CORRIDOR
Partly damaged

John Grimwade
Map of central Florence, created for *Condé Nast Traveler* using Adobe Illustrator. A basic street plan given a very effective 3-D treatment by the addition of simplified representations of key buildings, enhanced by cast shadows. Shadows are also used to great effect under the bridges.

Grundy & Northedge
A movie-goer's view of San Francisco, created for the London *Sunday Times* using Adobe Illustrator. A highly stylized treatment of a street map—although the grid layout of many American city streets can hardly be treated otherwise. This map is enhanced by the addition of silhouettes of key structures. The near geometric representation of the coastline gives an informal feel to the map.

bounford.com
Flow chart showing vehicle loading and offloading at the Channel Tunnel terminals, created for Eurotunnel plc using Macromedia FreeHand. A simplified map base orientates travelers embarking and disembarking at either end of the tunnel. The function of the diagram is to reassure passengers by demonstrating the simplicity of the procedures.

166

John Grimwade
Diagram describing how hurricanes happen, created for *Popular Science* using Adobe Illustrator. A fascinating composite of several diagrams— relational, statistical, and illustrative. This page demonstrates how well text and imagery can be integrated to make an engrossing information tableau.

AFRICAN RAINFALL AND HURRICANE FORMATION

20 WETTEST YEARS

20 DRIEST YEARS

More rain

RAINFALL IN SAHEL REGION YEAR-BY-YEAR

Average rainfall

More drought

1950 1955 1960 1965 1970 1975 1980 1985 1990

Whenever the hurricanes return, the damage will be much worse than in the '50s and '60s, because of the vast coastal development since then. Fully half the U.S. population now lives in East Coast areas prone to hurricane flooding. Insurance policies on

INSIDE A HURRICANE
Moisture spirals up within the eye-wall and returns as rainfall. As the storm intensifies, the column begins to spin faster and faster, sucking up more warm, wet winds. Inside the eye the winds rarely exceed 15 mph.

Outflow

Eye-wall

Rain bands

Eye

Inflow

GULF OF MEXICO

AFRICA

SAHEL REGION

CARIBBEAN SEA

EL NIÑO
This tropical Pacific current brings ultra-warm water east toward Central and South America every few years, generating high-altitude westerley winds that blow across Central America and prevent hurricanes from forming. The last few years have seen a string of El Niños that have kept most hurricanes at bay. But that, says Gray, is about to change.

WHERE HURRICANES FORM
Hurricanes start off the coast of western Africa as loose regions of bad weather known as tropical depressions. Wet weather in the Sahel region of Africa strongly influences how many depressions form in a given season. As they move across the Atlantic, some depressions intensify into more powerful tropical storms that circulate counter clockwise. If a tropical storm's sustained winds reach 75 mph, it

How Hurricanes Happen

Hurricanes start as "seedlings" off the coast of Africa, then gradually intensify as they cross the Atlantic. The two biggest contributors to a strong hurricane season are the El Niño Pacific Ocean current and, most important, heavy rainfall in the Sahel region of Africa.
But why does hurricane activity fall and rise in roughly 20-year cycles? William Gray theorises that oscillations in a worldwide current known as the "Great Ocean Conveyer Belt" are ultimately responsible for cycles in African rainfall, and hence hurricanes. Currently, we're overdue for another heavy-hurricane cycle.

THE GREAT OCEAN CONVEYOR BELT
Warm tropical water circulates up to the Arctic, then cools and sinks, and returns south.

WARM

COLD

When the conveyor belt is moving slowly, there is little wind and moisture to cause monsoons over west Africa, which stays warm and dry. Over years, the hot weather helps evaporate ocean water, creating salty, heavy water. When the salty water reaches the North Atlantic, it cools and sinks deeply, strengthening the cold water return of the belt. Gradually this speeds up the belt. A stronger belt whips up winds and moisture near Africa, spawning the Sahel rainstorms that ultimately escalate into hurricanes that head towards the U.S.

Less hurricanes

DEEP RETURN

WEAKER

More El Niño

More hurricanes

LESS RETURN

STRONGER

Less El Niño

Rowson Holbrook
Map showing railway track modifications on the North London line. Designed for the European Passenger Service. Created using Macromedia FreeHand. The point of the diagram was to show the intricate complexity of

re-engineering works on a busy section of London's overground railway system.

168

John Grimwade
Diagram and maps describing a damming project on China's Yangtze River, created for *Condé Nast Traveler* using Adobe Illustrator. Four map styles are employed here to give the reader a clear locational context

and to indicate the scale of the project. In the illustrative diagram a common element—the boat— is used to convey the immensity of scale.

Will China's heavenly river become the valley of the dammed?

Shibao Zhai Pagoda

RESERVOIR LEVEL

Water level will rise about 200 feet

TOWN

RIVER LEVEL NOW

The scale of the Three Gorges Dam, like everything else in China, is positively gargantuan. The project is expected to take 17 years to complete, the estimated cost is $36 billion, and 1.25 million people will be made homeless as a result. With the flooding of the valley, 13 cities, 140 towns, and 1,352 villages, in addition to thousands of historical and archaeological treasures, will be submerged. The reservoir created by the dam will wind westward, for a total of 370 miles. The fabled beauty of the Three Gorges—the Qutang, the Wu, and the Xiling—will be destroyed forever as the water level rises, and the ancient Shibao Zhai Pagoda (*left*), which now towers above the Yangtze, will soon find the river touching its base.

Tuotuoheyan

TIBETAN PLATEAU

UPPER SECTION

Wanxian

Fengjie

THE THREE GORGES

Towns that will be submerged

RESERVOIR

Present course of the Yangtze

Badong

Zigui

Shennong River

Zhongxian

Fengdu

QUTANG GORGE   WU GORGE

NEW DAM

Chongqing

Fuling

50   100   150   200

XILING GORGE

250 MILES

Existing dam
Yichang

MIDDLE   SECTION   AREA ENLARGED ABOVE

Daju

Lijiang

TIGER LEAPING GORGE

Wuhan

LOWER SECTION

Nanjing

100   200
MILES

Shanghai

EAST CHINA SEA

CHINA

Beijing

TIBET   YANGTZE

Shanghai

INDIA

Hong Kong

500 miles

Denver   Washington, D.C.

YANGTZE

500 miles

Dallas

SAME SCALE: The Yangtze River superimposed on the United States.

The river at the center of the world

From its source in the Tanggula Mountains in the Tibetan Plateau to its estuary, north of Shanghai, the Yangtze is more than 3,900 miles long. An icon of China's ancient civilization, the river is also its lifeline, covering 25 percent of the country's agriculturally viable land.

N

GRAPHICS by JOHN GRIMWADE

Nigel Holmes
A double-page spread from Richard Saul Wurman's book *Understanding USA*, illustrating US federal budget income and expenditure. The book is composed entirely of graphic spreads and contains no text. Created using Macromedia FreeHand. Skillful use of icons helps the reader assimilate a vast amount of detailed statistical information.

170

Individual
income tax
$899.7 billion

The tax levied on your salary and any other income you have, such as profits made on investments or interest earned on savings. It's a "progressive" tax, which means that the higher your income the greater percentage of it you'll pay to the government. Tax rates range from 15% to 39.6%.

47.8%

Corporate
income tax
$189.4 billion

A tax on corporate income. Rates range from 15% to 38%.

10.1%

Social
insurance tax
(FICA)
$636.5 billion

The Social Security and Medicare tax, which is withheld from your salary. The rate is 15%; half is paid by you and half by your employer. The self-employed pay the full 15% of their income themselves.

33.8%

Excise tax
$69.9 billion

A tax on goods such as tobacco and alcohol.

3.7%

Estate and
gift tax
$27.0 billion

Estate tax is levied on property at the time of death. Gift tax is due on large gifts.

Customs duty
$18.4 billion

A tax on certain imports coming into the U.S.

Miscellaneous
receipts
$42.1 billion

The Federal
government's
total income
for 2000
is projected to be
$1.9 trillion

The government's income in 2000 is **$1.9 trillion.**

From this income, two kinds of payment must be made:

①
Payments to mandatory entitlement programs

Mandatory spending is money the government spends automatically—unless the President and Congress change the laws that govern it.

②
Discretionary service payments

Discretionary spending is money the President and Congress must decide how to spend each year.

Numbers may not add up due to rounding

Medicare
$216.6 billion

Provides "universal" health insurance to nearly 40 million aged and disabled.

Funds to low-income earners
$274.6 billion

Includes federal grants for state welfare programs, federal low-income housing programs and funds for community and regional development in at-risk areas.

Social security
$408.6 billion

Provides income security to 48 million aged and disabled people. This is the single largest federal program, representing over 22% of our entire budget.

Veterans' benefits **$44.0 billion**

Health
$152.3 billion

Finances and provides health care services; aids disease prevention; supports research and training.

Interest on the National Debt
$215.2 billion

The amount paid by the federal government to service our $5.7 trillion debt. This is offset by interest collections from the public and interest received by government trust funds (such as *the Social Security Trust Fund). Net interest is very sensitive to interest rates and the amount of debt outstanding. Because rates are low, interest paid is expected to decrease about 5% from the 1999 level.*

National defense
$274.1 billion

Includes conventional forces, atomic energy defense, and other defense-related activities. Spending has decreased (in real terms) for most of the 1990s but will increase in 2000 to meet challenges of peace-keeping and terrorism.

International affairs **$16.1 billion**

Education **$63.4 billion**
Includes subsidies to elementary, secondary and higher education, and research.

General science, Energy, Environment, and Agriculture **$56.1 billion**
Includes space flight (NASA $650 million), high-tech research, and subsidies *to farmers and environmental conservation.*

Transportation **$46.4 billion**
Includes grants to states for subways and buses, water and air transport, *and subsidies to AMTRAK.*

General government and Administration of Justice **$42.0 billion**
Includes salaries of the President, the executive branch, legislators and judges.

Mandatory spending
$1.3 trillion

Discretionary spending
$0.5 trillion

So, in 2000, the U.S. will spend
$1.8 trillion...

... leaving about
$115 billion
over what was taken in as taxes. This is the projected surplus.

But...

bounford.com
Chart showing the global organization of advertising agencies. Created for *The Economist* magazine using Macromedia FreeHand. Color is used to identify "family" groupings, with colors blended to indicate joint interests. It will take many hours of preparation in order to resolve all the interrelationships in a chart like this.

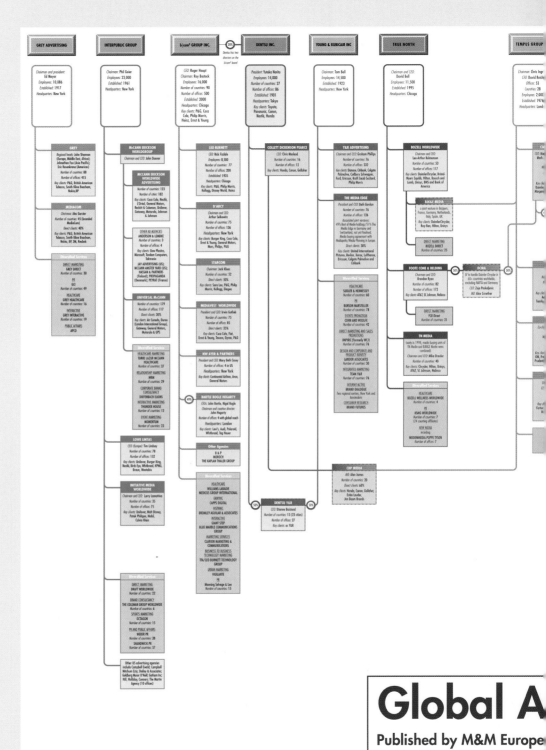

Global A

Published by M&M Europe

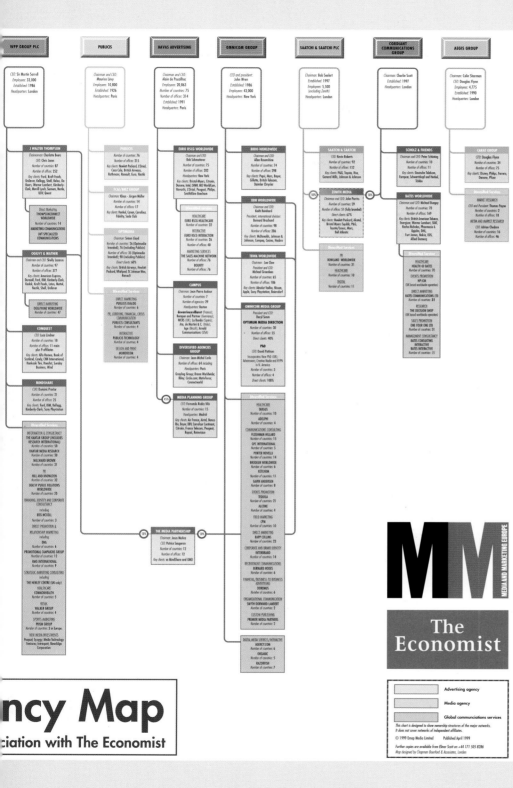

ncy Map

...ciation with The Economist

173

MM MEDIA AND MARKETING EUROPE

The Economist

Advertising agency

Media agency

Global communications services

This chart is designed to show ownership structures of the major networks.
It does not cover networks of independent affiliates.

© 1999 Emap Media Limited   Published April 1999

Further copies are available from Elinor Scott on +44 171 505 8286
Map designed by Chapman Bounford & Associates, London

John Grimwade
Diagrammatic map describing the North Atlantic air traffic system, created for *Condé Nast Traveler* using Adobe Illustrator. A highly complex combination of relational and organizational diagrams. The use of perspective and shading lends realism to the chart.

174

The Transatlantic Superhighway

EVERY DAY ABOUT 900 AIRCRAFT FLY
INSIDE THE NORTH ATLANTIC
ORGANIZED TRACK SYSTEM

The Concorde flies between 50,000 and 60,000 feet, far above the main traffic flow.

4 HALFWAY POINT
At 30°W, responsibility for the flight is transferred from Gander to Prestwick Oceanic Air Traffic Control in Scotland.

360 MILES

Some flight levels are reserved for aircraft flying in the direction opposite the peak flow.

3 POSITION CHECK
Aircraft in oceanic airspace are out of radar contact for about four hours. Position reports are made by radio at every 10 degrees of longitude, and the information is used to update displays at the oceanic control centers.

Aircraft crossing the main traffic flow (for example, Madrid to Los Angeles) are routed above or below the track system.

60 miles
80 miles
60 miles
80 miles (10 min.)
2,000 feet
2,000 feet

ORGANIZED TRACK SYSTEM

FLIGHT LEVELS (FEET)
39,000
37,000
35,000
33,000
31,000
29,000

2 SAFETY ENVELOPE
Aircraft must keep minimum distances from one another in the track system, while maintaining constant altitude and speed.

UNITED KINGDOM
Prestwick

SHANWICK OCEANIC CONTROL AREA

ICELAND

Shannon

IRELAND

GREENLAND

WESTBOUND (DAY)

GANDER OCEANIC CONTROL AREA

A B C D E

T U V W X

30°W

EASTBOUND (NIGHT)

EAST INTO THE NIGHT
As a result of passenger demand, time zone differences, and airport noise restrictions, North Atlantic air traffic has two peak flows: eastbound, leaving North America in the evening, and westbound, leaving Europe in the morning. Every 12 hours a new track system is prepared, to allow as many aircraft as possible to follow the most economical flight paths. Because of changing weather conditions, the track positions are rarely identical.

1 GETTING IN LINE
Taking into account airlines' preferred routes, oceanic controllers at Gander, Newfoundland, organize aircraft approaching from different directions into position for the Atlantic crossing. This flight is entering the system on track V at 35,000 feet.

CANADA

Gander

NEWFOUNDLAND

JET STREAM

NORTH ATLANTIC OCEAN

Graphics by
JOHN GRIMWADE

232

233

Grundy & Northedge
Diagram for British Nuclear Fuels annual report showing the workings of a nuclear generator, created using Adobe Illustrator. An organizational diagram which makes strong use of bright color and simplified graphics. By reducing the complex stages to highly stylized icons the physical structure and scale of the workings can be ignored, giving the reader a manageable understanding of the basic process.

175

from reaction to transmission

Fuel Delivery

Reactor

Turbine/condenser

Generator

Transformer/Grid

Users

The generating story

Control & Security

Boiler

Control rods

CO_2 gas

Graphite moderator

Boiler

Fuel elements

Gas circulator

Gas circulator

Concrete pressure vessel

Steel pressure vessel

Steam in

Turbine

steam out

Condenser

Cooling water pump

Water filter

2000 volts

Turned into current

Onto the national grid

Factory

Office

Home

1 2 3 4 5 6 7

GLOSSARY

adaptive smoothing In some drawing and 3-D applications, smoothing which is applied to a path only where it is required, rather than uniformly.

Adobe Acrobat Proprietary software that lets you convert any document into a PDF (portable document format) file, in which fonts and images are embedded, enabling it to be viewed on different computer systems.

airbrush/airbrushing A tool invented in the USA around 1900, used in illustration and photographic retouching, in which a fine spray of paint or ink is propelled by compressed air.

airbrush tool A tool used in some software programs to simulate the behavior and effect of a mechanical airbrush.

algorithm A predetermined procedure for solving a specific problem.

algorithmically defined Usually used to describe a font in which each character is drawn "on-the-fly" according to the calculations made by a software program, rather than residing on the computer as a predrawn font file.

aliasing The jagged appearance of bitmapped images or fonts occurring either when the resolution is insufficient or when the images have been enlarged. This is caused by the square pixels making up the image becoming visible to the eye. Sometimes called "jaggies," "staircasing," or "stairstepping."

angle of view The angle between opposite faces of a viewing pyramid (the structure created by drawing two lines from the center of a view to its edges). The more extreme the perspective, the greater the angle.

animation The process of creating a moving image by rapidly moving from one still image to the next. Traditionally, this was achieved through a laborious process of drawing or painting each "frame" (a single step in the animation) manually on to cellulose acetate sheets ("cels" or "cells"). However, animations are now more commonly created with special software which renders sequences in a variety of formats, typically QuickTime, AVI, and animated GIFs.

anomalous data Any data which looks to be at variance with the rest of its data set.

anti-aliasing A technique of optically eliminating the jagged effect of bitmapped images reproduced on low-resolution devices such as monitors. This is achieved by blending the color at the edges of the object with its background by averaging the density of the range of pixels involved. Anti-aliasing is also sometimes used to filter texture maps, such as those used in 3-D applications, to prevent moiré patterns.

area chart Chart that shows data values as an area.

aspect ratio The ratio of the width of an image to its height, expressed as x:y. For example, the aspect ratio of an image measuring 200 × 100 pixels is 2:1.

background The area of an image upon which the principal subject or foreground sits. It may be colored to give extra definition to the image.

bar chart/graph A chart or graph using bars to represent quantities.

baseline The line on the grid that indicates the starting point.

bas-relief An image which is embossed and stands out in shallow relief from a flat background, designed to give the illusion of further depth.

Bézier curve In drawing applications, a curved line between two "control" points. Each point is a tiny database, or "vector," which stores information about the line, such as its thickness, color, length, and direction. Complex shapes can be applied to the curve by manipulating "handles" which are dragged out from the control points.

binary An arithmetical system which uses 2 as its base, meaning that it can only be represented by two possible values—e.g., a 1 or a 0, on or off, something or nothing, negative or positive, small or large.

binary code The computer code, based on 1 or 0, which is used to represent a character or instruction. For example, the binary code 01100010 represents a lower case "b."

bit A commonly used acronym for binary digit, the smallest piece of information a computer can use. A bit is expressed as one of two values—e.g., a 1 or a 0, on or off, something or nothing, negative or positive, small or large. Each alphabet character requires eight bits (called a "byte") to store it.

bit map Any text character or image composed of dots. A bit map is a map describing the location and binary state (on or off) of bits, which defines a complete collection of pixels or dots that make up an image, such as on a display monitor.

bitmapped font A font in which the characters

are made up of dots, or pixels, as distinct from an outline font, which is drawn from vectors. Bitmapped fonts generally accompany Post-Script "Type 1" fonts and are used to render the fonts' shape on screen (they are sometimes called "screen" fonts). To draw the shape accurately on screen, your computer must have a bit map installed for each size (they are also called "fixed-size" fonts), although this is not necessary if you have Adobe Type Manager installed, as this uses the outline, or "printer" version of the font (the file that your printer uses in order to print it). TrueType fonts are "outline" and thus do not require a bitmapped version.

bitmapped graphic An image made up of dots, or pixels, and usually generated by "paint" or "image-editing" applications, as distinct from the "vector" images of "object-oriented" drawing applications.

Boolean The name describing a shorthand for logical computer operations, such as those which link values—"and," "or," "not," etc., called "Boolean operators." In 3-D applications, Boolean describes the joining or removing of one shape to or from another.

brief Written instructions detailing the parameters, scope, quality, and timing of a piece of work.

bump map A bitmap image file, normally grayscale, most frequently used in 3-D applications for modifying surfaces or applying textures. The gray values in the image are assigned height values, with black representing the troughs and white the peaks. Bump maps are used in the form of digital elevation models (DEMs) for generating cartographic relief maps.

byte A single group made up of eight bits (0s and 1s) which is processed as one unit. It is possible to configure eight 0s and 1s in only 256 different permutations, thus a byte can represent any value between 0 and 255—the maximum number of ASCII characters, one byte being required for each.

CAD (computer-aided design) Strictly speaking, any design carried out using a computer, but the term is generally used with reference to 3-D design, such as product design or architecture, where a computer software application is used to construct and develop complex structures.

camera-ready copy/art (CRC) Material, such as artwork, prepared and ready for photographic conversion to film in preparation for printing. Also called a "mechanical," "composite art," or "paste-up."

caption Strictly speaking, a headline printed above an illustration identifying its contents. Today, however, a caption is generally used to mean any descriptive text which accompanies illustrative matter, and should, more accurately, be described as a "legend."

caricature The depiction—as a photograph, model, or drawing—of a person or object with exaggerated key features or characteristics. Generally executed for comic or satirical purposes.

Cartesian coordinate system A geometry system employed in 3-D applications which uses numbers to locate a point on a plane in relation to an origin where one or more points intersect.

cartouche A decorative device, usually in the form of a scroll with rolled-up ends, which is used to enclose a title or illustration.

cause-and-effect diagram A pictorial representation of the analysis of a process, identifying the cause of a problem or the solution to it, and the effect that that may have on the process. Also called a "fishbone" diagram.

cell A single space or unit for entering data into rows and columns, such as in a spreadsheet.

clip art/clip media Collections of royalty-free photographs, illustrations, design devices, and other precreated items, such as movies, sounds, and 3-D wireframes. Clip art is available in three forms—on paper, which can be cut out and pasted onto camera-ready art, on computer disc, or, increasingly, via the Web.

clipboard The place in the memory of a computer where text or picture items are temporarily stored when they are copied (or cut). The item on the clipboard is positioned in an appropriate place when "Paste" is selected from the menu. Each process of copying or cutting deletes the previous item from the clipboard.

clipping Limiting an image or piece of art to within the bounds of a particular area.

clipping path A Bézier outline that defines which areas of an image should be considered transparent or "clipped." This lets you isolate the foreground object and is particularly useful when images are to be placed on top of a tint background in a page layout, for example. Clipping paths are generally created in an image-editing application such as Adobe Photoshop and are embedded into the image file when you save it in EPS format. Some page

180

layout applications, such as QuarkXPress, allow you to create clipping paths for images, but be warned: these are only saved with the application file, so if your placed images are low-resolution FPO files which are to be replaced by the high-resolution versions, or if they are the preview files of a five-file DCS (desktop color separation) file, your clipping path will not have any effect.

clipping plane In 3-D applications, a plane beyond which an object is not visible. A view of the world has six clipping planes: top, bottom, left, right, foreground, and background.

clone In image editing, to duplicate pixels in an image in order to replace defective ones, or to add to an image by duplicating parts of the same, or another, image.

column chart A vertical bar chart.

concertina bar diagram A bar diagram that compares three sets of data by adding the third set of data plots in the same plane as one of the data plots of a mirror bar chart.

constrain (1) A facility in some applications to contain one or more items within another. For example, in a page layout application, a picture box (the "constrained item") within another picture box (the "constraining box"). (2) In 3-D applications, to restrict an item to a particular plane, axis, or angle.

contour line A line on a map joining points of equal altitude.

control point In vector-based (drawing) applications, a little knob, or point, in a "path" (line) which enables you to adjust its shape or characterisics by means of "Bézier control handles."

controlling dimension One of the dimensions—either height or width—of an image, which is used as the basis for its enlargement or reduction in size.

crosshatch A line drawing style in which tonal variations are achieved by groups of parallel fine lines, each group being drawn at a different angle.

cross section An illustration of an object that shows it as if sliced through with a knife, thus exposing interior details or workings.

crow quill A very fine ink pen, deriving from the days when scribes used the cut quill of a crow to write with.

cubic mapping In 3-D applications, the technique of applying one copy of a texture map (image) to each of the six sides of a cube.

cutaway An illustration of an object in which part of its outer "shell" has been removed to show the inner workings or details.

cutout A halftone image in which the background has been removed to provide a freeform image. Also known as an "outline halftone" or "silhouette halftone."

cylindrical (map) projection A map projection in which all lines of longitude ("meridians") run parallel with each other and at right angles to the lines of latitude ("parallels"). Cylindrical projections are highly distorted at the Polar extremities but, when wrapped around a sphere, appear normal and are thus ideal for use with 3-D applications. Cylindrical projections are widely used for navigation purposes and thus for navigational graphics. "Gall" and "Mercator" are typical cylindrical projections,

named after the men who devised them.

cylindrical mapping In 3-D applications, the technique of applying a texture map (image) to a cylindrical 3-D object, such as applying a label to a bottle.

data graphic Any visual representaion of data.

data point The precise value used in plotting a line graph.

degradé/degradee A graded halftone tint which, by varying the dot size, gradually changes from one edge to the other.

delineate To emphasize outlines in line drawings or artwork by making them heavier.

digital Anything operated by or created from information or signals represented by binary digits, such as a digital recording. As distinct from analog, in which information is represented by a physical variable (in a recording this may be via the grooves in a vinyl platter).

digital dot A dot generated by a digital computer or device. Digital dots are all the same size whereas halftone dots vary in size, so in digitally generated halftones many dots—up to 256 (on a 16 x 16 matrix)—are required to make up each halftone dot.

digital elevation model (DEM) A collection of regularly spaced elevation data from which 3-D models of the earth's surface can be generated. DEMs are used extensively by cartographers to produce shaded relief maps using special software.

dingbats The modern name for fonts of decorative symbols, traditionally called printer's ornaments, flowers, or arabesques.

181

dot A term which can mean one of three things: halftone dot (the basic element of a halftone image), machine dot (the dots produced by a laser printer or imagesetter), or scan dot (strictly speaking, pixels, which comprise a scanned bitmapped image). Each is differentiated by being expressed in lpi (lines per inch) for a halftone dot, dpi (dots per inch) for a machine dot, and ppi (pixels per inch) for a scan dot—although the latter is sometimes expressed—erroneously—in dpi. Thus, because the term "dot" is used to describe both halftone and machine dots, scan dots should always be referred to as pixels.

dot/stripe pitch The distance between the dots or pixels (actually, holes or slits in a screen mesh) on your monitor—the closer the dots, the finer the display of image.

double rule The term used to distinguish two lines of different thickness (in traditional typesetting, made from brass) from two lines of the same thickness, called a "parallel rule."

draw(ing) application Drawing applications can be defined as those which are object-oriented, using vectors to mathematically define lines and shapes, as distinct from painting applications, which use pixels to make images (bitmapped graphics). Some applications combine both functions.

drop shadow A shadow projected onto the surface behind an image or character, designed to lift the image or character visually off the surface.

elevation The drawn vertical projection of an object, typically front, side, or end.

ellipse An oval shape which corresponds to the oblique view of a circular plane.

embossing (1) Relief printing or stamping in which dies are used to impress a design into the surface of paper, cloth, or leather so the letters or images are raised above the surface. (2) Simulation of this effect on a computer.

end cap In drawing applications, the method in which the end of a line or an object is rendered; in 3-D applications, the closing of an open end left by a lathe, sweep, or extrude operation.

engraving (1) A block or plate made from wood or metal into which a design or lettering has been cut. (2) A print taken from an engraved print or block. (3) Computer simulation of this effect.

error diffusion In digital scanning, the enhancement of an image by averaging the difference between adjacent pixels. In graphics applications this technique is more commonly referred to as "anti-aliasing" which, in turn, uses a technique known as "interpolation."

exploded view An illustration of an object displaying its component parts separately—as though it were exploded—but arranged in such a way as to indicate their relationship within the whole object when assembled.

extrude The process of duplicating the cross-section of a 2-D object, placing it in a 3-D space at a distance from the original and creating a surface which joins the two together. For example, two circles that become a tube.

fall off In a 3-D environment, the degree to which light loses intensity away from its source.

feather(ing) The gradual fading away of the edge of an image or part of an image to blend with the background. Feathering tools are a feature of image-editing and painting applications.

fill In graphics applications, the contents, such as color, tone, or pattern, applied to the inside of a closed path or shape, including type characters.

fill characters The characters inserted between specified tab stops in some applications.

fine rule A rule, traditionally of hairline thickness. In graphics applications this can mean a rule of any thickness between 0.20–0.50 points, but which is invariably defined as 0.25 points. (see *also* **hairline rule**)

flow chart A diagrammatic representation of a process.

free-form shape A shape that is not regular or geometric.

fresnel factor In a 3-D environment, the brightening of the edge of an object by increasing the intensity of reflection along the edge, giving a more realistic visual effect.

ghosting An illustration technique in which the outer layers of an object are faded to reveal its inner parts, which would not normally be visible. The technique is used particularly in technical illustration. e.g., to show parts of an engine covered by its casing.

Gouraud shading In 3-D applications, a method of rendering by manipulating colors and shades selectively along the lines of certain vertices, which are then averaged across each polygon face in order to create a realistic light and shade effect.

182

graphic device Any illustration or drawn design.

graph paper Special paper marked with a series of very fine and thicker lines for the purposes of precise plotting and drawing of graphs.

graticule A grid system of lines used to provide reference points on an image, particularly the lines of latitude ("parallels") and longitude ("meridians") on a map.

grid In some applications, a user-definable background pattern of equidistant vertical and horizontal lines to which elements such as guides, rules, type, boxes, etc., can be locked, or "snapped," thus providing greater positional accuracy.

ground plane In some 3-D applications, a reference plane oriented on the x–z axis, providing a reference for the ground.

guides In many applications, nonprinting horizontal and vertical lines which can be placed at inconsistent intervals and which help you to position items with greater accuracy.

hachures Parallel lines used in hill-shading on maps, their closeness indicating the steepness of gradient.

hairline rule Traditionally, the thinnest line that it is possible to print. In applications which provide a size option for rules, it is usually 0.25 points wide.

high-profile Any item which stands apart or visibly proud of its surroundings.

high-resolution monitor Monitor capable of displaying 24-bit color.

histogram A graphic representation of data, usually in the form of solid vertical or horizontal bars. Some image-editing applications use histograms to graph the number of pixels at each brightness level in a digital image, thus giving a rapid idea of the tonal range of the image so that you can tell if there is enough detail to make corrections.

icon In a computer "graphical user interface," a graphic representation of an object, such as a disc, file, or tool, or of a concept or message.

ideogram A symbol used to indicate a concept or emotion, such as joy, sadness, or warmth.

illuminate/illuminated The technique of embellishing letters, pages, manuscripts, etc., by using gold, silver, and colors, common in medieval times.

inked art Camera-ready art which is prepared first in pencil and then completed in ink.

intersection In some drawing and page layout applications, a feature that allows you to create a shape from two (or more) others that overlap or intersect each other.

intrinsic mapping In 3-D applications, a method of mapping a texture to a surface using the object's own geometry as a guide to placement rather than the geometry of another shape such as a cylinder or sphere.

isometric Where the plane of projection is at equal angles to the three principal axes of the object shown.

isotype A method for graphically presenting statistical information in which pictograms or ideograms are used to convey meaning, a technique pioneered by Otto and Marie Neurath's Isotype Institute.

jointed leader line Line with two angles to reach awkward points when linking annotation/caption to part of an illustration.

key An explanatory list of symbols or color coding used on a map, graph, chart, or any representation of information in visual form.

keyline A line drawing indicating the size and position of an illustration in a layout.

keyline view In some applications, a facility which provides an outline view of an object or illustration without showing attributes such as colors and line thicknesses.

leader(s) A row of dots, dashes, or other characters, used to guide the eye across a space to other relevant matter. In some applications, leaders can be specified as a "fill" between tab stops in text.

leader line/leader rule A line keying elements of an image to an annotation or a caption.

linear motion style In 3-D applications, a calculation of the unknown values between two known keyframe values of an animation based on calculating the shortest distance between the two.

line tool In graphics applications, the tool used to draw lines and rules. If the tool can only draw horizontal and vertical rules it is usually called an "orthogonal" line tool.

logarithm A figure representing the power to which a fixed number or base must be raised to produce a given number. Used to simplify calculations as the addition and subtraction of logarithms is equivalent to multiplication and division.

logarithmic scale A scale based on logarithms. These never start from zero, and can be in any base but base ten is the most frequently used.

matrix A rectangular array of elements in rows and columns that is treated as a single entity.

median The middle value of a series of values arranged in order of size.

midtones/middletones The range of tonal values in an image anywhere between the darkest and lightest, usually referring to those approximately halfway.

mirror bar chart A bar chart that compares two sets of data where they are placed on either side of a baseline.

mitred/mitre The beveled ends of right-angled frame rules used in traditional typesetting. Also used in software applications as a method of defining the "end caps" in rules or lines.

mono(chrome)/monochromatic An image of varying tones reproduced in a single color.

multiple graphs Graphs which show the plots of several sets of data, used for comparison of similar data.

negative value Values less than zero, to be subtracted from others or from zero.

normal(s) In 3-D objects, the direction that is perpendicular to the surface of the polygon to which it relates.

oblique projections Projections rendered with one plane of the object drawn head on, and the receding planes angled to one side. Although any angle other than 90° can be used, 45°, 30°, and 60° are the most common.

one-point perspective Projection with one vanishing point.

orthographic (projection) An illustration technique in which there is no perspective (or the perspective is infinite), thus giving parallel projection lines.

outline font A vector-based digital font drawn from an outline which can be scaled or rotated to any size or resolution, as distinct from "bitmapped fonts" comprised of pixels and used primarily for screen display in the case of Post-Script fonts. Also called "printer fonts" or "laser fonts" (because they are essential for rendering fonts accurately when output on laser printers and imagesetters), or "scaleable fonts."

Oxford corners A box rule where the lines project beyond the frame corners.

Oxford rule The combination of a thick and a thin rule.

paint(ing) applications Applications which use bitmaps of pixels to create images rather than the vectors that describe lines in drawing applications (called "object-oriented"), though some applications combine both.

PANTONE® The proprietary trademark for Pantone Inc.'s system of color standards, control, and quality requirements, in which each color bears a description of its formulation (in percentages) for subsequent printing. The PANTONE MATCHING SYSTEM® is used throughout the world so that colors specified by any designer can be matched exactly by any printer.

parallax The apparent movement of two objects relative to each other when viewed from different positions.

parallel rule The term used to distinguish a rule composed of two lines of the same thickness (made from brass in traditional typesetting) from one composed of two lines of different thickness, called a "double rule."

Pareto diagram A diagram which illustrates the theory (the "Pareto principle") that 80 percent of the effects of a situation come from only 20 percent of possible causes.

peaking A method of digitally sharpening images by using a filter that increases the difference in density where two tonal areas meet. Also called "sharpening edges."

perspective A technique of rendering 3-D objects on a 2-D plane, duplicating the "real world" view by giving the same impression of the object's relative position and size when viewed from a particular point—the shorter the distance, the wider the perspective; the greater the distance, the narrower the perspective.

phong shading A superior but time-consuming method of rendering 3-D images, which computes the shading of every pixel. Usually used for final 32-bit renderings.

pictogram/pictograph A simplified, pictorial symbol distilled to its salient features to represent an object or concept.

pie chart An illustration which shows the divisions of a whole quantity as segments of a circle or ellipse.

pitch In 3-D construction, the rotation around the x-axis.

184

pixel Acronym for picture element. The smallest component of a digitally generated image, such as a single dot of light on a computer monitor. In its simplest form, one pixel corresponds to a single bit; 0 = off, or white, and 1 = on, or black. In color or grayscale images or monitors, one pixel may correspond to several bits: an 8-bit pixel, for example, can be displayed in any of 256 colors (the total number of different configurations that can be achieved by eight 0s and 1s).

pixelation An image that has been broken up into square blocks resembling pixels, giving it a "digitized" look.

plot area The area of a graph defined by the data. The area containing the data points.

point In object-oriented drawing applications, the connections ("Bézier points") which mathematically define the characteristics of line segments, e.g., where they start and end, how thick they are. (Each point is a vector or tiny database of information). Lines are manipulated by dragging "control handles" (sometimes called "guidepoints") from the point, which act on the line like magnets.

point markers In line graphs these are used to mark the position of the precise data values used to plot the line.

polygon The smallest unit of geometry in 3-D applications, the edges of which define a portion of a surface.

polygon resolution The detail in a 3-D scene defined by the number of polygons in a surface, which, in turn, determines the detail of the final rendering—the more polygons, the finer the detail.

polygon tool A tool in some applications with which you can create irregular-shaped boxes, in which text, pictures, or fills can be placed.

polyline In 3-D applications, a line with more than two points which defines a sequence of straight lines.

polymesh A 3-D object comprising shared vertices in a rectangular shape.

primitive The basic geometric element from which a complex object is built.

projection mapping Texture mapping onto a 3-D object where the texture appears to project through the image surface.

puck The more complex "mouse" used in CAD systems.

radial fill A feature of some applications in which an item can be filled with a pattern of concentric circles of graduated tints.

raster image An image defined as rows of pixels or dots.

raster(ization) Deriving from the Latin word "rastrum," meaning "rake," the method of display (and of creating images) used by video screens and computer monitors, in which the screen image is made up of a pattern of several hundred parallel lines created by an electron beam "raking" the screen from top to bottom at a speed of about one-sixtieth of a second. An image is created by the varying intensity of brightness of the beam at successive points along the raster. The speed at which a complete screen image, or frame, is created is called the "frame" or "refresh" rate.

rate determining factor (RDF) The rate at which progress is determined, defined as the slowest part of any procedure or process. For example, the rate at which you may be able to complete a design job will depend on how long it takes the slowest contributor (an author or illustrator, for example) to complete his or her task, in which case that person is the rate determining factor. It could even be you.

raytracing Rendering algorithm which simulates the physical and optical properties of light rays as they reflect off a 3-D model, producing realistic shadows and reflections.

readability The ease and comfort with which text can be read.

reflection tool In some applications, a tool for transforming an item into its mirror image, or for making a mirror image copy of an item.

relational diagram A diagram, for example, a map or a plan, showing the relative association of objects in the physical world.

relief map A cartographic map in which elevation is rendered to simulate three dimensions.

render(ing) The process of creating a 2-D image from 3-D geometry and applying lighting effects and surface textures to it.

rescale To amend the size of an image by proportionally reducing its height and width.

reverse image An image that has been reversed, either horizontally or vertically, so that what was on the left of the image is now on the right, or what was at the top is now at the bottom, as in a mirror image.

reverse out/reverse type To reverse the tones

of an image or type so that it appears white (or another color) in a black or colored background. Also called "dropout," "save out," or "knockout."

roll In a 3-D environment, the rotation of an object or camera around the z-axis.

rotation tool In some graphics applications, a tool which, when selected, enables you to rotate an item around a fixed point.

roughness map In some 3-D applications, a texturing function to control surface roughness.

rule A printed line. The term derives from the Latin "regula," meaning "straight stick," and was used to describe the metal strips of type height, in various widths, lengths, and styles, which were used by traditional typesetters for printing lines.

ruler In some applications, the calibrated ruler at the edges of a document window, in a preferred unit of measure.

ruler guide In some applications, a nonprinting guide which you position by clicking on the ruler and dragging it to the desired location.

same size (S/S) An instruction that original artwork/illustrations should be reproduced without enlargement or reduction.

sample size The number of pixels, or the amount of data, used as a sample to assess information about an image or about other digital files, such as sounds.

scale an animation To lengthen or shorten the length of time of an animation.

scale/scaling The process of working out the degree of enlargement or reduction required to bring an image to its correct reproduction size.

scale drawing A drawing, such as a map or plan, which represents the subject matter in proportion to its actual size and to a specified scale. For example, an object drawn to a scale of 1:10 means that one unit of measurement on the drawing is equivalent to 10 of the same units on the object at full size—so one inch on the drawing equals 10 inches at full size.

scan dot The resolution of a scanning device, measured—like machine dots—in dots per inch. However, the formula for calculating scan dot resolution does not relate to that of calculating machine dot resolution. A rough rule of thumb is that for images that will eventually be printed with a halftone screen ruling greater than 133lpi, the scan resolution should be 1.5 times the lpi screen ruling, and for screens equal to, or less than, 133lpi, the scan resolution should be 2.0 times the lpi ruling. Scanning at higher resolutions will not make any difference because the halftone dots will not be small enough to reproduce the extra detail.

scatter diagram/graph A graph used to analyze the cause-and-effect relationship between two variables where two sets of data are plotted on x and y axes, the result being a scattering of unconnected dots.

score In some 3-D applications, the term describing time information about each object and property in a scene.

screen ruling In halftone screens, the number of ruled lines per inch or centimeter. The greater the number, the finer the resolution. The range in common use varies from 85lpi for halftones printed on newsprint to 150lpi or more for those printed on art papers.

sepia A brown color and also a monochrome print in which the normal shades of gray appear as shades of brown.

shading In 3-D applications, the resulting color of a surface due to light striking it at an angle.

shadow (area) The areas of an image which are darkest or densest.

sharpen(ing) Enhancing the apparent sharpness of an image by increasing the contrast between adjacent pixels.

skew(ing) A feature built into some graphics applications allowing type characters or images to be slanted. Also known as "shearing."

skin In 3-D applications, a surface stretched over a series of "ribs," such as an aircraft wing.

smoothing The refinement of bitmapped images and text by a technique called anti-aliasing (adding pixels of an "in-between" tone). Smoothing is also used in some drawing and 3-D applications, where it is applied to a path to smooth a line, or to polygons to tweak resolution in the final rendering.

smooth point A Bézier control point which connects two curved lines, forming a continuous curve.

snap to In many applications, a facility that automatically guides the positioning of items along invisible grid lines, which act like magnets, aiding design and layout.

specular map In 3-D applications, a texture map—such as those created by noise filters—which is used instead of specular color to control highlights.

specular reflectance The reflection (as by a mirror) of light rays at an angle equal to the angle at which it strikes a surface (angle of incidence).

spherical map(ping) In 3-D applications, a technique of mapping a rectangular image to a sphere—the rectangle first becomes a cylinder, which is then wrapped around a sphere by pinching the top and bottom of the cylinder into single points, or "poles."

spline The digital representation of a curved line that is defined by three or more control points, common in 3-D applications.

split bar chart A chart where the individual components in a bar are broken down into their individual parts and labeled. The component bars are placed end to end, either as a vertical column chart or horizontal bar graph. Also known as a stacked bar.

spotlight In 3-D applications, a beam of light shown as a cone.

spreadsheet An application that allows you to make complex calculations encompassing almost any user-defined criteria. A spreadsheet uses a table of rows and columns, and the spaces in the grid, known as cells, can be moved and mathematically manipulated. Some spreadsheet applications will also generate graphics (3-D in some cases) from the data entered into the cells.

square corner tool A feature of most graphics applications, used for drawing squares and rectangles. Also called a "rectangle tool."

stacking order The position of items relative to others, in front or behind, in software.

starburst In some applications, the shape that the pointer assumes when certain transformation tools are selected.

stippling An illustration technique by which an image is composed of repeated small dots of ink or paint applied with a fine-tip pen or brush.

stylize/stylization The imposition of a graphic style on an image, as distinct from a realistic representation of it.

surface In 3-D applications, the matrix of control points and line end points underlying a mapped texture or color.

surface geometry In 3-D applications, the geometry that underlies a surface, becoming visible when the surface is simplified.

symbol A figure, sign, or letter that represents an object, process, or activity. A computer icon, for example, is a pictorial symbol.

symmetrical point A Bézier control point that connects two curved lines, forming a continuous curve. Also called a "curve point."

table A set of facts or figures displayed systematically, particularly in columns.

tangent line In a 3-D environment, a line passing through a control point of a spline at a tangent to the curve. The tangent line is used to adjust the curve.

taper Referring to graduated tones and colors, the progression of one tone or color to the next.

taper angle The direction in which graduated tones or colors merge into one another.

template (1) A shape used as a drawing aid. (2) A document created with prepositioned text and images, used as a basis for repeatedly creating other similar documents.

texture mapping/surface mapping In 3-D environments, the technique of wrapping a 2-D image around a 3-D object.

3-D Three dimensional, that is, an effect to give the illusion of depth on a flat page or monitor.

three-point perspective A projection with three vanishing points.

tile/tiling The repetition of a graphic item, with the repetitions placed side-by-side in all directions so that they form a pattern—just like tiles.

tilt In a 3-D environment, a camera that performs vertical pans (up and down) about its horizontal axis.

topographic structure A detailed description of the natural and artificial features of a terrain.

tracking The adjustment of space between characters in a selected piece of text. As distinct from "kerning," which involves only pairs of characters.

transformation tool In some applications, the name given to tools that change the location or appearance of an item, such as "scale" or "reflection."

transposing (1) Exchanging the position of any two items of text, or two images. (2) In a bar chart, shifting the alignment of the bars.

trend line In a scatter graph, a line drawn through a concentration of data points to pick it out.

trim curve In a 3-D environment, a curve on the surface of one object where it is intersected by another, allowing you to trim away parts of the surface.

tritone A halftone image that is printed using three colors. Typically, a black-and-white image is enhanced by the addition of two colors, for example, when added to black, process yellow and magenta will produce a sepia-colored image.

uniform smoothing In some 3-D applications, uniform smoothing converts the surface of a model into a grid of evenly spaced polygons.

union In drawing applications, the combining of two or more shapes into one.

up vector In a 3-D environment, a line perpendicular to the viewpoint of a camera that allows the camera object to be rolled around the viewpoint.

u-v coordinates In a 3-D environment, a system of rectangular 2-D coordinates used to apply a texture map to a 3-D surface.

vector Information giving both magnitude and direction.

vector drawing program A program that uses mathematical points to define lines and shapes.

velocity In 3-D animation, the rate of change in an object's location relative to time.

vertex In a 3-D environment the x, y, and z locations at each corner of a polygon or control point.

vertex animation In 3-D animation, varying the shape of an object by animating its surface control points.

vertical alignment The placement of items, such as images or lines of text, in relation to the top and bottom of a page, column, or box.

vertical centering The equidistant positioning of text ("vertical justification") or any other item from the top and bottom of a page, column, or box.

viewpoint In a 3-D world, the position of the viewer relative to the view.

volume chart Used for comparing data vastly different in value, and for representing large data. Because it uses three dimensions as opposed to two, it can represent values up to ten times the size of those represented by an area chart without occupying more space.

x, y coordinates The point—e.g., on a graph, monitor, or bitmap—at which data is located on 2-D axes: horizontal (x) and vertical (y). 3-D coordinates are known as "x, y, z coordinates" (or axes).

yaw In a 3-D environment, rotation around the y-axis.

z-buffer renderer A 3-D renderer which solves the problem of rendering two pixels in the same place (one in front of the other) by calculating and storing the distance of each pixel from the camera (the "z-distance"), then rendering the nearest pixel last.

zero base The horizontal line which cuts across the y-axis at value zero. Any value above the zero base is a positive value; any value below the zero base a negative one.

INDEX

ACKNOWLEDGMENTS

MAY 1 8 2004

We are grateful to the following for their kind help and for allowing their work to be included in this volume.

John Grimwade for "Round-the-World Balloons" and "How Hurricanes Happen" from *Popular Science*, "Pipe Organ" from *Smithsonian* magazine, "New York Grand Central Station," "Angkor Wat," "Map of Florence," "The Yangtze River," and "North Atlantic Air Traffic" from *Condé Nast Traveler*; Grundy & Northedge for "Heading Icons" from *Bloomberg* magazine, "Icons"' from the *Camelot Annual Report*, "Five Financial Crashes" from *Worldlink* magazine, "Movie-goer's View of San Francisco" from *The Sunday Times*, and "How Nuclear Generators Work" from the *British Nuclear Fuels Annual Report*; Nigel Holmes for "Diagram of Breast Examination" from *Self* magazine, "Greg Louganis's Reverse Pike Dive" from *Olympic Dreams* (Rizzoli), "Map of the Brain" and "The Bombing of the Uffizi Gallery" from *Time* magazine, "Gas Engine" from *Attaché* magazine, and "The National Debt" and "US Federal Budget" from *Understanding USA* (TED Conferences Inc.); Bill Le Bihan for the "Four Stroke Engine Cycle"; Annabel Milne for "Teeth Cleaning" and "Angiogenesis" from the *Antisoma Prospectus*; and Rowson Holbrook for "Map of a Railway Track Modification for the North London Line."

Although every effort has been made to trace copyright owners, there may be a few instances where this has proven impossible. We would like to take this opportunity to apologize to any copyright holders whose rights we may have unwittingly unfringed.